THE SCOTTISH PULPIT

FROM

THE REFORMATION TO THE PRESENT DAY

THE
SCOTTISH PULPIT

FROM

THE REFORMATION

TO

THE PRESENT DAY

BY

WILLIAM M. TAYLOR, D.D., LL.D.

AUTHOR OF

"PETER THE APOSTLE," "DAVID, KING OF ISRAEL,"
"JOSEPH, THE PRIME MINISTER," ETC.

Solid Ground Christian Books
Birmingham, Alabama

SOLID GROUND CHRISTIAN BOOKS

PO Box 660132, Vestavia Hills, AL 35266

205-443-0311

sgcb@charter.net

http://www.solid-ground-books.com

The Scottish Pulpit
from the Reformation to the Present Day

by William M. Taylor (1829-1895)

Taken from the 1887 edition by Charles Burnet & Co., London

Published by Solid Ground Christian Books

Classic Reprints Series

First printing February 2004

ISBN: 1-932474-27-7

Manufactured in the United States of America

TO

THE MEMBERS OF THE FACULTY

OF THE

THEOLOGICAL DEPARTMENT OF YALE UNIVERSITY

AND THE STUDENTS UNDER THEIR CARE

These Lectures

DELIVERED AS THE LYMAN BEECHER COURSE FOR 1886

Are Dedicated

WITH HIGHEST REGARD BY

THE AUTHOR

PREFACE.

THE design of these sketches is neither to give a full account of Scottish Ecclesiastical History nor to furnish complete biographies of the men who have been prominent in the Scottish Pulpit since the Reformation. My aim has simply been to put the preachers in the environment of their times, to bring out the characteristics by which they were distinguished, and to give point to such lessons from their work as may be useful in our own age.

The form in which the sketches are presented was determined by the fact that they were originally addressed to the students of Yale Theological Seminary in the spring of 1886, when I had the honour of holding, for the second time, the appointment of "Lyman Beecher Lecturer" in that institution.

For reasons which are too obvious to need to be formally stated, I have not attempted to deal with living Scottish preachers, many of whom are worthy of a place beside the foremost of those whom I have specified; and if some names which might have been expected to find a place in such a review as I have attempted are not referred to, I hope that the limits within which I felt myself restricted in such a brief course will be deemed sufficient to account for the omission.

The facts given and the dates mentioned have in all cases been faithfully verified, but it is scarcely possible that no error has crept in, especially as so many works—most of them, alas!—without any index, had to be searched for the purpose of insuring accuracy.

I have to acknowledge my obligation for valuable hints as to sources of information which I received from my honoured friends, Principal Cairns, of Edinburgh; Professor William Graham, of the Presbyterian College, London; and President McCosh, of Princeton.

The preparation of the volume has been throughout a labour of love, into which perhaps there has entered also somewhat of national enthusiasm and pride; and if it shall prove in any way serviceable to the great cause to which I have given my life, I shall be abundantly rewarded.

WM. M. TAYLOR.

5 WEST THIRTY-FIFTH STREET,
    New York, 1887.

CONTENTS.

CHAP.		PAGE
I.	INTRODUCTORY AND HISTORICAL	1
II.	JOHN KNOX AS A PREACHER	37
III.	MELVILLE.—RUTHERFURD.—DICKSON.—LIVINGSTONE	63
IV.	ARCHBISHOP LEIGHTON.—THE FIELD PREACHERS	105
V.	THE MODERATES AND EVANGELICALS	139
VI.	THOMAS CHALMERS	185
VII.	THE PULPITS OF THE DISSENTING CHURCHES	221
	INDEX	269

THE SCOTTISH PULPIT

FROM

THE REFORMATION TO THE PRESENT DAY.

I.

INTRODUCTORY AND HISTORICAL.

FOR an intelligent appreciation of the Scottish Pulpit we must have some knowledge of the Scottish character, and some acquaintance with at least the main lines of Scottish Ecclesiastical History.

Between the people and the pulpit of a nation action and reaction are continuously operative. Originally a man of the people, partaking in all their national peculiarities, and educated in the midst of them, the preacher has been largely moulded by what they are; while, on the other hand, his influence tends to modify their disposition, and in all times of crisis and agitation becomes a potent factor in the settlement of affairs.

The leaves put forth by a tree do at length fall from it and fertilize its roots; and the pulpit, which is very largely the fruit of a nation's life, comes ultimately to affect that life. Or, to borrow the illustration of Mr. Gladstone, the preacher receives from the people in vapour that which he gives back to them in flood, but that flood carries them away with it to enterprises which else they had never undertaken. So in entering upon our theme we must pause for a few moments to speak of the distinctive features of the Scottish people.

These are not difficult to discover. Foremost among them—indeed the very vertebral column of the national character—is sturdy independence. The Scotsman insists upon the right to be, and to belong to, himself. He will let no one think for him or dictate to him. This came out in the patriotic and political struggles of the people, and also, as we shall see, in their ecclesiastical conflicts. But it is just as characteristic of the individual as it is of the nation as a whole. Their great poet has at once expressed and strengthened it by the lyric fervour of the glowing song in which these words occur:

> "The rank is but the guinea's stamp,
> The man's the gowd for a' that."

Everywhere the people are jealous of any interference with the great human birthright of private judgment. The very national motto, with its distinct individuality, "Nemo *me* impune lacessit," is an assertion of this quality, and occasionally it has run to seed into controversies which have brought it well-nigh into ridicule. The youth who, when asked why he was going to the debating society, answered, "Oh, jist to contradic' a wee," was perhaps an exaggerated specimen, but the right to have, to maintain, and to act upon his own conviction is one which every true Scotsman would defend to the utmost.

Behind this independence, as the hot-blast to the furnace, is that intensity which has become proverbial as the "præfervidum ingenium Scotorum," and which makes him terribly in earnest in everything that he does. It acts upon him as a convex lens does on the rays of the sun, focussing him upon that which he undertakes until it bursts into a flame which may either kindle a holy enthusiasm or a destructive conflagration.

Then, strangely enough, in connection with that fervour there is a persistence amounting almost to dogged stubbornness which keeps the Scotsman steadily at a thing until he has gained his end.

This quality of "*dourness*"—to give it the vernacular name—makes the true Caledonian everywhere pertinacious. He rarely, if ever, lets go that of which he has taken hold, and all that he enters upon he carries through. He has what I may call the spirit of "stick-to-it-iveness" in perfection; and that was a wise prayer which he is said to have offered on one occasion: "Lord, grant that we may be right, for thou knowest we are very decided."

Happily, with this indomitable firmness there is combined a very large measure of caution, or what is commonly ridiculed as "*canniness.*" He leaps with intensity, but he looks before he leaps. He stands *like* a rock, because he has first taken care to stand *on* a rock. The high average of intelligence in the nation consequent upon its excellent system of education enables him to see with clearness where the right lies, and so his persistence, which might otherwise have been fraught with mischief, has been mainly an immense power for good.

Then there is in him a poetic sense which enables him to appreciate the ideal, and halos even common things for him with "the light which never was on sea or land." That had its bright efflorescence and

INTRODUCTORY AND HISTORICAL.

undying illustration in Robert Burns; for he was exceptional only in the fact that his genius enabled him to express the feelings which were struggling for utterance in his countrymen, and to bring into light the poetry that was already lying latent in their lives. In him it was creative, in them it is receptive; but it is in them, else they could not appreciate him as they do—well-nigh to the verge of idolatry; and they who are most conversant with the peasantry of the land will confirm me when I say that in their ordinary conversation there is not a little of that richness of simile and that spirituality of insight which we associate with poetry.

Add to these a humour of a quaint, sometimes grim, and occasionally playful sort; not often boisterous, but when it is, shaking the sides with laughter; frequently sly, or, as they call it, "*pawkie*," and when there is need, stinging and sarcastic too. Some one has said that it requires a surgical instrument to get a joke into the head of a Scotsman, but that is a libel on the people which probably was never meant to be seriously understood; and every intelligent reader of Dean Ramsay's book will know what value to put upon the assertion. Perhaps the author of it had forgotten to make allowance for the fact that, as a rule, the Scotch are undemonstrative, and would not be apt to show always that they did appreciate a joke. And that reminds me to mention, as a feature too important to be lost sight of in our present department, the reticence, especially in regard to sacred things, by which they are characterized. Even in secular affairs they

> " Still keep something to theirsel's
> They scarcely tell to ony; "

but this reserve is more marked in spiritual matters. They feel a great deal more than they say, and they are disposed to regard almost as irreverent any common reference to personal religious experiences in the presence of others.*

Some of these qualities have been modified in recent years, but as a rule they are still very largely characteristic of Scotsmen generally, and we shall find continual illustrations of their influence on their greatest preachers, at well as in their Ecclesiastical History. Indeed, this last department,

---

* This was well illustrated by the remark of the good old gentlewoman who said to her young friend, when broaching the subject of spiritual experience on the street, "Whist, lassie; they are no causey cracks"—*i.e.*, subjects for street gossip.

INTRODUCTORY AND HISTORICAL. 7

owing very largely to that sturdy individual independence of which we have spoken, is to the uninitiated a labyrinth in which they speedily lose themselves; and even those who are at home in such matters find it a tangled skein, requiring both skill and patience for its unravelment. Happily for our present purpose, all that is necessary is some general acquaintance with "the lie of the land," together with an accurate knowledge of its watersheds and divisions.

Speaking generally, then, we may say that modern Scottish Church History may be divided into three periods, each remarkable for its own conflict running through it, and terminating with its own victory. They may be styled the periods of anti-popery, anti-prelacy, and anti-patronage. The first of these, beginning with Patrick Hamilton, had its formal termination in 1567, when the Act of Parliament which established Protestantism in the country was put upon an unquestionable foundation. To this period belong the names of Hamilton, Wishart, and Knox—by the last of whom, especially, the Reformation was effected and the Protestant Church organized after the type of Genevan Presbyterianism.

The anti-prelatic period began almost immediately

after the death of Knox, in 1572, and continued, in one form or another, until the Revolution, in 1688. Its earliest phases was closely connected with—indeed almost grew up out of—the unwise arrangement which had been made in the matter of the temporalities of the Roman Church, when it was disestablished at the Reformation. Greatly to the mortification of Knox, who wished to devote the larger part of them to education, these were divided into three parts, of which two were secured for life to the Popish incumbents who had been displaced, and one was divided between the Court and the Protestant ministers. When, however, these Romish life-renters died, the question arose what was to be done with their emoluments, and the greedy nobles, eager to get hold of them, fell upon a scheme by which they might gain their end. They claimed the right of presentation to the benefices, and put into them under the old titles men who had first pledged themselves to keep only a percentage of the incomes, and pass the rest on to their patrons. The presentees had the names and the lords had the money, and so the people, with a dash of that humour to which I have referred, called them "tulchan" bishops—a tulchan being the name given among them to the skin of a calf stuffed with straw and set up beside a

INTRODUCTORY AND HISTORICAL.

cow to induce her to give her milk more freely into the dairymaid's pail. All this was ludicrous enough, but it was the insertion of the thin end of the wedge, and many efforts were made at a later date to drive it home. When King James, Sixth of Scotland and First of England, came—I was going to say to years of discretion, but he never really came to them, though he was styled "the wisest fool in Christendom;" let me rather say—to mature age, he sought, with intervals of vacillation, to act upon his favourite maxim, "*No bishop; no king.*" By the issuing of edicts, the prohibition of the holding of meetings of the General Assembly of the Church, the appointment of bishops, and the banishment of the Presbyterian leaders from their native land, he endeavoured to force Episcopacy on Scotland. But the people were unwilling to receive it, and he left his project as a legacy to his son Charles. To this section of the anti-prelatic period belong the names of Andrew Melville, John Welsh, and others.

When, in 1625, Charles the First came to the throne, he entered with zest upon the work which his father had been prosecuting, and calling to his aid Archbishop Laud, he pushed matters to extremities with an issue that was disastrous mainly to himself. The act of Jenny Geddes, in 1637, when, in the old cathedral of St. Giles, she threw her stool at the head of the Dean of Edinburgh as he began to read the collect for the day from the new liturgy, which was to be forced upon the people by the sole authority of the king, and without any consultation with them, was the spark that kindled materials already collected for the fire which burned on until the Stuarts were banished from the throne, and their divine right nonsense was finally exploded. Whether such a liturgy should be used or not was perhaps no great thing to dispute about. Opinions will differ as to that. But whether a liturgy of any kind, or, for that matter, anything at all, should be forced from without on a people without any consultation with them, and whether they would have it or not—*that* was a great question, involving in it the liberty of the nation ; and to divert attention from that to the bigotry, as some call it, of those who could dispute over the reading of a collect is to evade the issue, and mistake entirely the temper of the men who raised it. People do not call John Hampden stingy because he refused to pay the few shillings which were demanded of him as ship-money by the king without the concurrence of Parliament. It was not a matter of shillings, but of constitutional

INTRODUCTORY AND HISTORICAL. 11

right, and in refusing to yield he stood upon the principle which secured the independence of these United States—no taxation without representation. The difference between liberty and slavery may turn upon a little thing, but it is not a little difference; and in this case the *émeute* in which the apple-woman of the High Street of Edinburgh played such a prominent part led on and up to the Parliamentary struggle and the Civil War which cost Laud and Charles their heads, and culminated, for the time, in the Commonwealth and Protectorate of Cromwell. To this stage of the anti-prelatic conflict belong the names of Alexander Henderson, Samuel Rutherfurd, and George Gillespie, men not unworthy to be the coadjutors of Selden, Vane, Howe, Calamy, and others in England. "There were giants in those days upon the earth," and these were of them. Here also come in the signing of the National Covenant in 1638, the adoption of the Solemn League and Covenant in 1643, and the sitting of the Westminster Assembly of Divines during the years 1643–1649.

Under Cromwell, who was himself an Independent, the Scottish Church, from 1651 to 1658, was neither Prelatic nor Presbyterian. He dissolved the General Assembly with as little ceremony as he did the Long Parliament, and exercised autocratic power in a manner that brooked no interference with his commands. But, as one has said, "The despot was intelligent and benevolent, and no earnest minister was suffered to be molested while engaged in any spiritual work." *

When, however, at the Restoration in 1660, the Stuart dynasty returned to the throne in the person of Charles the Second, the cave of Æolus was once more opened, and

> "Una, Eurusque Notusque ruunt creberque procellis
> Aquilus."

Everything that had been undone was done again more offensively than before. Bishops were sent down from England to push Episcopacy on the land; ministers who would not conform were ejected from their parishes; the people were forbidden to worship elsewhere than in the churches; and those who adhered to the Covenant took to the glens and the moors, where they held their conventicles in defiance of the law, thereby entailing upon themselves cruelties which can be paralleled only by the deeds of the Inquisitors of Spain or the

---

* "Handbook of Scottish Church History," page 65. N. L. Walker.

INTRODUCTORY AND HISTORICAL. 13

Dragonnades of France. These were the times of persecution,

" Whose echo rings through Scotland to this hour,"

and which lasted through the reigns of Charles the Second and James the Second, till the day on which William of Orange landed at Torbay, on the invitation of the great majority of the English people, to take the throne of their nation at the most critical moment of its history. To this section of the anti-prelatic period belong such men as Cameron, Cargill, Renwick, on the one side, and, singularly enough, a saint like Archbishop Leighton on the other. But at its close prelacy received its death-blow in Scotland, where, ever since, it has been in the main an exotic, needing the protection of the conservatory to keep it from the keen climatic winds.

The Revolution settlement of Scottish ecclesiastical matters, however, was not absolutely satisfactory to any party, but it was accepted by all save the rigid "Society-men," or Cameronians, as the best which could be obtained under the circumstances. It was the result of multitudinous negotiations between William and the Scottish leaders, and was comprised in several Acts of the Scottish

Parliament. It abolished Episcopacy, repealed the statute by which the royal supremacy in the Church had been established; restored the ministers who had been ejected in 1662; opened the way for the retention of such of the Episcopal clergy as were willing to conform to Presbyterianism; and legalized the Westminster Confession of Faith as that of the Scottish Church. Over lay patronage—that is, the vesting in laymen, principally landowners, of the right of appointing ministers to congregations—the new king hesitated longest, and on that the whole matter had nearly suffered shipwreck. William was a latitudinarian, or perhaps, more correctly, an indifferentist, in Church government; but he was a stickler for patronage, regarding it as property belonging to the patrons which should not be interfered with. At length, however, he gave way so far as to consent that—the patrons being compensated in money for what he counted their loss—the right of proposing a minister should be vested in a parochial council consisting of the Protestant landowners and the elders of the parish, while the congregation should have liberty to object to the person proposed, and the Presbytery was authorized to determine the validity of the objections. The union of England and Scotland came in 1707, and by the

INTRODUCTORY AND HISTORICAL. 15

Act of Security it was ordained that the Confession of Faith and the Presbyterian form of government should "continue without any alteration to the people of the land in all succeeding generations." In spite of that guarantee, however, the Government of Queen Anne, in 1712, introduced into Parliament and carried a measure which took the power of electing ministers from the parochial councils, and vested it in the ancient patrons, being the Crown for above five hundred and fifty livings, and gentlemen of landed property, town councils, &c., for the remaining five hundred. To this enactment all the secessions from the Scottish Church, as by law established, are directly to be traced.

The result of the Revolution settlement was that at the beginning of the eighteenth century the clergy of the Church were made up of what Dr. McCosh has called* " a somewhat heterogeneous mixture of Covenanting ministers who had lived in the times of the persecution; of Prelatic clergy, whose convictions in favour of Episcopacy were not sufficiently deep to induce them to abandon their

---

* "The Scottish Philosophy," p. 17. James McCosh, D.D., LL.D.

livings; and of a race of young men zealous for the Presbyterian establishment, but only 'half-educated and superficially accomplished.'" The amalgam proved to be a type of preachers who called themselves Moderates, and ultimately became the dominant party in the Church; when, as Witherspoon said, they showed themselves "very immoderate for moderation." In their discourses the more highly educated of them cultivated the graces of literature and rhetoric to a great degree of excellence, but avoided all distinctively evangelical topics, and confined themselves to the truths which are common to both natural and revealed religion. They were tolerant of everything but evangelical enthusiasm, and it is not uncommon that ministers were placed by them over congregations who were so unwilling to receive them that the military had to be called out to preserve the peace during the installation services. For nearly a hundred years they carried matters with a high hand, and the consequence of their ascendancy was—I quote again from McCosh—that "the common people in rural districts sunk into a stupid ignorance of religious truth, and, in the crowded lanes of the rising cities, into utter ungodliness and criminality, except in so far as" these evils were counteracted " by the

INTRODUCTORY AND HISTORICAL. 17

rapidly increasing Dissenters, or by the Evangelical minority within the Established Church." *

But there was always a "remnant" which was true to the doctrines of grace, and at length the members of that "old guard," led by Sir Henry Moncreiff, Dr. Andrew Thomson of Edinburgh, and afterwards by Dr. Thomas Chalmers, increased in numbers to such an extent that they became the majority. This created a great spiritual revival over the land, led to extraordinary efforts for what Chalmers called the "excavation" of the heathen at home; to the inauguration of missionary enterprise among the heathen abroad; and ultimately, through an effort to get rid of the evils of patronage, and the interference of the civil courts with the spiritual independence of the Church, issued in the memorable Disruption of 1843, when, rather than submit to things which were declared to be inseparable from their connection with the State Church, more than four hundred ministers left their manses and their churches, and formed the Free Church of Scotland. To this period belong, on the Moderate side, William Robertson, the historian; Hugh Blair, the rhetori-

---

* The Scottish Philosophy," p. 18. James McCosh, D.D., LL.D.

cian; Principal Hill, the theologian; Alexander Carlyle, commonly known as Jupiter Carlyle, and others; and on the Evangelical, Dr. John Erskine, the correspondent of Jonathan Edwards; John Maclaurin, John Witherspoon, Andrew Thomson, Thomas Chalmers, and his trusty lieutenants, Candlish, Cunningham, Buchanan, and Guthrie. It may be said to have come to an end with the passing of Disraeli's bill for the abolition of Patronage in 1874; but within these recent years another period, which will be known in history as the Anti-State-Church period, has begun, and of that we may say that the issue is not doubtful, though it may not be immediate.

I have confined myself thus far, for the sake of clearness, to the direct course of the Established Church; but now I must go back and trace the rise and progress of the Dissenting denominations. The Cameronians, or Society-men, known more lately as the Reformed Presbyterian Church, never entered into the Church of the Revolution settlement. They insisted that the monarch and people should accept and subscribe to the National Covenant, and because they could not secure that, they declined to perform all the duties of citizenship,

INTRODUCTORY AND HISTORICAL.

though they maintained a high standard of religious character. Their Church never grew into much strength, and latterly the larger number of their congregations united with the Free Church, leaving not more than half a score—if so many—to perpetuate the name.

The first Secession dates from 1733, and is connected primarily with the name of Ebenezer Erskine. In that year a sermon was preached by Mr. Erskine, as retiring moderator of the Synod of Perth and Stirling, in which he protested, both eloquently and forcibly, against the evils then existing in the Church, and especially against that of Patronage. For this he was by the Synod pronounced worthy of censure, and on appeal to the General Assembly he was, along with three other brethren who by that time had placed themselves by his side, summarily cast out of the Church, These four formed themselves into a Presbytery, and proclaimed the right of the members of the Church to choose their own ministers and office-bearers. By the year 1747 they had grown into a denomination of forty-five congregations; but at that date an unhappy controversy arose among them over the lawfulness of taking an oath which was administered to those who became burgesses in certain cities and towns of the country, and which pledged the obtestant to uphold "the true religion presently professed within the realm." This was supposed by some to refer simply to the Protestant religion, and those who were of that opinion believed that any Seceder might take the oath; but by others it was held to signify the Established Church of the country, and those who maintained that construction believed that no Seceder could consistently come under such an obligation. Between these two parties the contention was so sharp that they parted asunder the one from the other, and the former were popularly known as *Burghers*, the latter as *Anti-Burghers*.* These two denominations grew up side by side, holding no communion with each other, until in a spring-tide of prayerful fellowship they

---

* These names have been much ridiculed, and often very greatly misunderstood. An amusing instance of misapprehension regarding one of them may here be given. Some twenty years ago, or more, an application was made to a benevolent committee in Edinburgh on behalf of a lady in reduced circumstances, described as "the daughter" of an Anti-Burgher minister. The late Bishop Terrot, who was presiding, said, in all good faith, "Gentlemen, I have lived many years in Scotland, but I am ashamed to say I need to ask, *Where* is Anti-Burgher?" The *naïveté* with which the good bishop, while confessing to one sort of ignorance manifests another still more dense, is exceedingly delicious.

came together again in 1820, and formed the United Secession Church, which numbered at that date two hundred and sixty-two congregations, and continued to increase until, in 1847, it aggregated more than four hundred congregations.

Meanwhile a second secession from the Established Church had taken place. It was called the Relief Church, and had its origin, in 1752, in the deposition of Thomas Gillespie, minister of Carnock, for refusing to obey the order of the General Assembly commanding him to take part in the settlement over the parish of Inverkeithing of a minister who was obnoxious to the people. Gillespie meekly retired to Dunfermline, where he gathered round him a congregation, and where for six years he stood alone without any ecclesiastical connection. At the end of that time he was joined by Thomas Boston, son of the author of "The Fourfold State," and in 1761 a Presbytery was formed which took the name of Relief, because its purpose was to furnish "relief" to those churches into which pastors had been violently intruded by Patronage enforced through the civil law. This purpose it carried out so effectively that in 1847 it numbered seven Presbyteries, with an aggregate of one hundred and fourteen congregations; and in that year these two bodies—the United

Secession and the Relief—came together and formed what is now known as the United Presbyterian Church of Scotland. These churches, even in their separate state, exercised a great influence over the land. They kept the lamp of truth aflame in many parishes where but for them its rays had never shone, and the freedom of their environment allowed room for development. Adopting at first from necessity the practice of supporting their ministers by the free-will offerings of the people, they came at length to the perception of the truth that this is the normal state of a Church's life; and now, as a matter of fact, though it is not a term of communion among them, they are almost without exception the advocates of Anti-State-Churchism. They have outgrown, also, very largely the narrowness of mistaking points for principles. The Relief Church was the first Presbyterian Church in Scotland to introduce the singing of hymns into the worship of the congregation; and the United Church has led the way in the modification of subscription to creeds by the adoption of a declaratory statement which interprets the sense in which the Westminster Confession is accepted.* The next union will probably be between

---

* See note on p. 34: Declaratory Act of the United Presbyterian Church.

INTRODUCTORY AND HISTORICAL. 23

the United Presbyterian and Free Churches; and if the Anti-State-Church movement should be successful, it is not impossible that after the wounds of the conflict have been healed, the union may include also that which is now the Established Church.

To the dissenting bodies whose course I have thus sketched belong the Erskines, Ralph and Ebenezer; the John Browns, father, son, and grandson; George Lawson, John Dick, William Anderson, David King, John Eadie; and among living preachers, John Cairns, John Ker,* and others, who have contributed largely

---

* I leave this name to stand in the text as it was originally written, though now, alas! Dr. Ker has passed away, to the great grief of the entire Scottish nation. His volumes of sermons may give to readers on both sides of the Atlantic some idea of the place which he held as a preacher, but only those who knew him in the familiar intercourse of private life can form any adequate conception of the fulness of his information on all subjects, the soundness of his judgment, the warmth of his heart, the fineness of his humour, or the depth of his pathos. It was worth going a long way to hear him read some of the old metrical Psalms; and those who ridicule these productions would have altered their opinion could they have listened to his recitation of them. As to his discourses, great as they are, their greatness is not that of effort, for he never seems to be putting forth his whole strength in them. They have all the ease of spontaneity; they are, as it were, an efflorescence exhaling of itself, and revealing something still greater in the man himself.

to the homiletical and theological literature of their native land.

All these denominations came directly out of the Established Church, retaining the Westminster Confession as their doctrinal standard, and the Presbyterian polity as their form of government. It was otherwise, however, with the Congregationalism whose existence in Scotland began about the commencement of this century. It arose in the north of Scotland, as Dr. Alexander* says, "not in consequence of any departure on the part of its leaders from the doctrinal standards of the Established Church, nor from any speculative preference of a different form of church polity from that which hereditary attachment and the memory of past struggles and endurance, as well as conscientious conviction, had so endeared to the people of Scotland. . . . Theirs was from the beginning a movement of a purely spiritual kind. Like Methodism in England, the secession which they headed had its source simply in a craving for more life, more energy, more spiritual freedom and diffusiveness, than they could find in existing systems. They felt a need for a higher kind of spiritual

---

* "Memoir of Ralph Wardlaw, D.D.," p. 38. W. L. Alexander, D.D.

nourishment than they had been accustomed to, and for more of warmth and heartiness in the proclamation of religious truth to men, than the fashion of pulpit addresses at that time permitted."

The men who were most prominent in this movement were the brothers Haldane. Mr. James A. Haldane, who had been a sea-captain, but had grown into very intense spiritual convictions, came out as a lay-preacher, and visited several districts of the country, addressing immense multitudes of people, and awakening much spiritual interest by his fervent evangelical discourses. Mr. Robert Haldane promoted the same cause by the erection of suitable places of worship, the support of preachers in them, and the institution of a seminary for the training of ministers. Rowland Hill, Matthew Wilks, and others, came from England to their assistance. Crowds attended wherever they preached, so that they had often to meet in the open air, and sometimes as many as from fifteen to twenty thousand persons were computed to be present. This drew upon them the antagonism of some of the other denominations, notably the Established Church and the Anti-Burgher and Relief Synods, and their independent position was in a manner forced upon them by this lack of wisdom in the older bodies. Their success is thus accounted for by Dr. Alexander in a passage which I quote, not only for its bearing on the matter in hand, but also because it incidentally corroborates from another point of view some of the statements which I have made in other connections.

"In the National Church the long reign of Moderatism had done much to extrude all vital godliness, and to reduce the Christianity of both pastors and people to the lowest degree of attenuation compatible with the retention of the name. The majority of the ministers were avowedly Arminian, if not Pelagian, in their doctrinal views; not a few of them were Crypto-Socinians, and it was even insinuated that some holding no mean place in the Church were more than imbued with the scepticism of Hume. A few noble spirits still held aloft the banner of Evangelical orthodoxy, and stood valiantly by it, but they formed so slender a proportion of the whole that their efforts could do comparatively little towards counteracting the unwholesome influence of the majority. In the Dissenting Churches the state of things was undoubtedly greatly better, for in them no toleration was given to unsound doctrine, and the tone of religious sentiment and feeling was much higher than in the Establishment. Still there was but little of energetic piety even among them ; little of aggressive activity

INTRODUCTORY AND HISTORICAL. 27

in the propagation of the Gospel; little of what Shaftesbury derisively and yet most truly called 'the heroic passion of saving souls'; and along with this there was a much too prevalent disposition to set the mere apparatus of ecclesiastical order above the great ends for which such alone is valuable. And as religion shared in the general apathy amid which the eighteenth century was advancing to its close, so it shared, also, in that sudden awakening which the startling events in the neighbouring country [*i.e.*, France] had produced. Men, roused out of their long repose, became painfully aware of necessities which craved immediate relief. They felt that hunger of soul for suitable spiritual food which naturally follows a long period of spiritual destitution or inadequate supply. And as the existing ecclesiastical bodies were not sufficiently elastic—did not quickly enough expand—to meet the new and enlarged capacities and wants of the people, the latter impetuously rushed forth to find elsewhere what was denied them at home. Hence the crowds that followed Messrs. Haldane and Aikman on their first tours of preaching through Scotland. Hence the thousands upon thousands that covered the slopes of the Calton Hill to listen to the preachers from England; and hence the almost instantaneous rise into considerable strength of a new religious body hitherto nearly unknown in Scotland, and for which, as subsequent events proved, the Scottish mind was not in reality cordially prepared. The new wine could not be stayed in the old bottles, and so when it burst forth it was caught and kept by those who alone at the time were prepared to receive it." *

As the remark of Dr. Alexander near the close of the above extract confesses, Congregationalism has not grown into great proportions in Scotland, though for the year 1886-1887 I find one hundred churches returned; but no review of the Scottish Pulpit can afford to leave out the denomination which numbered among its preachers such men as Wardlaw and Alexander.

In the wake of the revival out of which Congregationalism arose in Scotland a Baptist controversy sprung up, and in many of the towns Baptist churches were formed; but although some of the preachers of that denomination have attained to honourable place, it cannot be said that the denomination, at least until very recently, has greatly

---

* "Memoir of Ralph Wardlaw," *ubi supra*, pp. 43, 44.

flourished in Scotland. In many places its members evinced a disposition to dispute over little matters, which led to divisions and subdivisions, while some of them adopted views opposed to the payment of pastors and the education of the ministry, which led among them to a "small-meeting-ism" not unlike that of the Plymouth Brethren in England. The Baptist Union of Scotland reported, however, in 1884 an aggregate of eighty-nine churches, and that organization is becoming a worthy sister of its English namesake.

The Evangelical Union had its origin in the Atonement controversy which shook the United Secession Church for years in the fifth decade of this century, and in the very hottest stage of which James Morison, now so widely known as one of our greatest New Testament exegetes, was deposed from the ministry for holding opinions on the extent of the Atonement, the Divine decrees, and the work of the Holy Spirit, akin to those of the Cumberland Presbyterian Church of America. He was joined by some ministers of the Secession Church who sympathized with his views, and by fifteen students who had been expelled from the Congregational Theological Seminary for maintaining the same doctrines.

This new organization speedily instituted a theological seminary, and now it numbers about a hundred churches, which are independent in government. It is not improbable that in the course of time this denomination and that of the Congregationalists will become one.

Such is a brief outline of the course of Church History in Scotland since the Reformation. I have not mentioned one or two of the smaller bodies lest I should confuse you by going too minutely into detail; but I have said enough to make intelligible to you those incidental references which must be inevitable in the prosecution of our special theme, and I conclude this prefatory lecture with a description of the curriculum of study required by these different denominations as preparatory to entrance into the ministry.

With the single exception of those small Baptist churches to which I have referred, and which are gradually disappearing, they are all alive to the importance of an educated ministry. There have been exceptional times and cases in the history of each of them when a university course or a theological training—properly so called—was dispensed with; but all the Presbyterian bodies require a full Arts course of four years at one or other of the National Universities, and in addition each insists upon a three years' course at its own Theological Seminary. Up till 1876 the Theological Seminary of the United Presbyterian Church, alike in its separate branches and in its united state, held its sessions for only two months of the year, and students were required to attend it for five sessions; while during the other ten months of these years they were under the care of their respective Presbyteries, before which they had to perform specified exercises, undergo prescribed examinations, and preach a certain number of discourses. This plan was suited to the circumstances of the students in the early history of these denominations, and enabled them to support themselves by teaching or otherwise in the intervals between the sessions. But in the year above specified the United Presbyterian Church came into line with its sister denominations, and now its professors hold no pastoral charge and teach for five or six months annually.

The Congregationalists and Evangelical Unionists do not count a University curriculum essential, though they prefer that it should be taken, and the seminary of the latter still follows the old Secession plan of a two months' session. Bursaries or scholarships are provided in the universities and in the seminaries, and are allocated for the most part by competitive examination; but they are few in number compared with the number of students. There are no Education Societies such as we have in this country, and students have to push their way as best they can, without the help that flows on this side of the water from these sources; but that does not keep them back, and there are few chapters of "Selp-Help" more heroic and spirit-stirring than those which the histories of the early struggles of many of our Scottish clergy would supply. The result has been what we may call "a survival of the fittest." The men who have gone through such a pathway to the ministry are apt to stay in it when they get there, and they are pretty sure to be heard from to some purpose. Such a biography as that of Dr. Robertson, first of Errol and afterwards of Edinburgh, from the pen of the accomplished Dr. Charteris, is typical of multitudes; and the early struggles of Thomas Carlyle on his way to his life work were no greater, and no more resolutely and bravely battled through, than those of many who have said far less about them, and have made their way to the foremost pulpits of their own or other lands. Indeed, most of the Scottish clergy might adopt the words of Edmund Burke with but a single change, and say: " I was not swaddled and rocked and dandled into a minister. 'Nitor in adversum' is the motto for a man like me." But they have not been the worse for that; nay, they have been all the better for that, since, knowing what struggle is, they have been so much the abler to speak " words in season " to those who are struggling, and that has been one element of their power.

NOTE. (See p. 22.)

Declaratory Act of the United Presbyterian Church.

As this Declaratory Act is the earliest attempt on the part of any Presbyterian Church to define the sense in which the Westminster Standards are understood to be subscribed by its office-bearers, and as it is not very widely known on this side of the Atlantic, we give it here in full:

"*Whereas* the formula in which the Subordinate Standards of this Church are accepted requires assent to them as an exhibition of the sense in which the Scriptures are understood: *Whereas* these Standards, being of human composition, are necessarily imperfect, and the Church has already allowed exception to be taken to their teaching or supposed teaching on one important subject: And *whereas* there are other subjects in regard to which it has been found desirable to set forth more fully and clearly the views which the Synod takes of the teaching of Holy Scripture: *Therefore,* the Synod hereby declares as follows:

" 1. That in regard to the doctrine of redemption as taught in the Standards, and in consistency therewith, the love of God to all mankind, His gift of His Son to be the propitiation for the sins of the whole world, and the free offer of salvation to men without distinction on the ground of Christ's perfect sacrifice, are matters which have been and continue to be regarded by this Church as vital in the system of Gospel truth, and to which due prominence ought ever to be given.

" 2. That the doctrine of the Divine decrees, including the doctrine of election to eternal life, is held in connection and harmony with the truth that God is not willing that any should perish, but that all should come to repentance, and

INTRODUCTORY AND HISTORICAL.

that He has provided a salvation sufficient for all, adapted to all, and offered to all in the Gospel; and also with the responsibility of every man for his dealing with the free and unrestricted offer of eternal life.

"3. That the doctrine of man's total depravity, and of his loss of 'all ability of will to any spiritual good accompanying salvation,' is not held as implying such a condition of man's nature as would affect his responsibility under the law of God and the Gospel of Christ, or that he does not experience the strivings and restraining influences of the Spirit of God, or that he cannot perform actions in any sense good; although actions which do not spring from a renewed heart are not spiritually good or holy—such as accompany salvation.

"4. That while none are saved except through the mediation of Christ, and by the grace of His Holy Spirit, who worketh when and where and how it pleaseth him; while the duty of sending the Gospel to the heathen, who are sunk in ignorance, sin, and misery, is clear and imperative; and while the outward and ordinary means of salvation for those capable of being called by the Word are the ordinances of the Gospel; in accepting the Standards, it is not required to be held that any who die in infancy are lost, or that God may not extend His grace to any who are without the pale of ordinary means, as it may seem good in His sight.

"5. That in regard to the doctrine of the Civil Magistrate, and his authority and duty in the sphere of religion, as taught in the Standards, this Church holds that the Lord Jesus Christ is the only King and Head of the Church, and 'Head over all things to the Church, which is His Body'; disapproves of all compulsory or persecuting and intolerant principles in religion; and declares, as hitherto, that she does not require approval of anything in her Standards that teaches, or may be supposed to teach, such principles.

"6. That Christ has laid it as a permanent and universal obligation upon His Church, at once to maintain her own ordinances, and to 'preach the Gospel to every creature'; and has ordained that His people provide by their free-will offerings for the fulfilment of this obligation.

"7. That, in accordance with the practice hitherto observed in this Church, liberty of opinion is allowed on such points in the Standards not entering into the substance of the faith, as the interpretation of the 'six days' in the Mosaic account of the creation: the Church guarding against the abuse of this liberty to the injury of its unity and peace."

The following question of the formula contains the terms in which the Subordinate Standards are accepted by the office-bearers of the Church: "Do you acknowledge the Westminster Confession of Faith and the Larger and Shorter Catechisms as an exhibition of the sense in which you understand the Holy Scriptures, this acknowledgment being made in view of the explanations contained in the Declaratory Act of Synod thereanent?"

II.

JOHN KNOX AS A PREACHER.

WE begin with JOHN KNOX, not only because through his instrumentality under God the Reformation in Scotland was mainly secured, but also because there are traces of his influence as a preacher to be discovered in the discourses of his successors down almost to the present day. He inaugurated a style which to the readers of these times seems much less antiquated than that of some subsequent periods, because at every era of crisis and revival in the land the earnest evangelical leaders who sought to conserve what he had gained went back to him as their model, and drew inspiration from his works. His "History of the Reformation" holds its place to this day among the books in the "cupboard libraries" of the Scottish peasantry, and even so lately as the time of the Disruption a volume of selections from his writings had a circulation of forty-four thousand copies, principally among the same class. Nor is it difficult from the study of these to discover in what particulars he, as it were, set the fashion for the preachers who came after him. But before we attempt to point these out we must first mark well the genesis of this particular method in himself, and for that purpose we need to take a brief review of his personal history.

Knox did not become a preacher until he had attained the age of forty-two. Born in 1505, he is found among the incorporated students of the University of Glasgow in 1522; and after his education was finished he seems to have entered the priesthood of the Roman Catholic Church, and to have continued in it up, at least, to 1543, for his name is found as notary affixed to a document which is still extant, and which bears that date. His first known public appearance on the side of Protestantism was in the beginning of 1546, when he attended George Wishart to Haddington as the bearer of a large two-handed sword to protect him from assault. His proper vocation, however, at this time was that of a teacher of youth, and to that, at Wishart's entreaty, he returned on the night of that martyr's apprehension. Up to that date, therefore, he had not entered upon the Protestant ministry, and as the manner of his call thereto had much to do with

JOHN KNOX AS A PREACHER. 39

the power of his preaching all through his later life, we cannot afford to ignore it in this place.

It was " on this wise." After the assassination of Cardinal Beaton the Castle of St. Andrews remained for a season in the hands of the men who had planned and carried out the " removal " of that prelate. It thus became a place of refuge for the Protestants, even if they did not all approve of the deed which had given them possession of the stronghold. Knox had nothing to do with the murder of the Cardinal, but for his own safety and that of his pupils he took them with him into the Castle of St. Andrews about the Easter of 1547, and there conducted his regular tutorial work with them from day to day. What that was he has thus described : " Beside their grammar and other humane authors he read unto them a catechism, an account whereof he caused them to give publicly in the parish church of St. Andrews. He read, moreover, unto them the Gospel of John, proceeding where he had left off at his departure from Longniddry, where before his residence was, and that lecture he read in the chapel at a certain hour." These public exercises were regularly attended by a large number of those who were sojourning within the castle, and the result was that Henry Balnaves, a distinguished Scottish priest, Sir David Lindsay the poet, and others, recognizing his fitness for the work, urged him most earnestly to enter on the ministry of the Gospel. But he strenuously refused, declaring that "he would not run where God had not called him." They were not, however, to be thus gainsaid, and therefore they arranged that on a certain day John Rough, who was pastor of the Castle church, should, in the name and behalf of the church, give him unexpectedly a public call to the ministry. So, after having preached a sermon on the election of ministers, Rough, in the presence of all the congregation, turned to Knox and said: "Brother, ye shall not be offended; albeit that I speak unto you that which I have in charge, even from all those that are here present, which is this: In the name of God and of His Son Jesus Christ, and in the name of those that presently call you by my mouth, I charge you that ye refuse not this holy vocation, but that, as ye tender the glory of God, the increase of Christ's kingdom, the edification of your brethren, and the comfort of me, whom you understand well enough to be oppressed by the multitude of labours, that ye take upon you the public office and charge of preaching, even as ye look to avoid God's heavy dis-

JOHN KNOX AS A PREACHER.

pleasure, and desire that He shall multiply His graces with you." Then turning to the congregation, he said: "Was not this your charge to me?" They answered: "It was, and we approve it." The suddenness and solemnity of this call thoroughly unmanned Knox, who burst into a flood of tears, and hastened to his closet, where we may well believe that he sought light from God. The result was that he was led to take up that work which he laid down only with his life. Not from the impulse of caprice, or because he desired the position of a preacher, but because he could not otherwise meet the responsibility which God had laid upon him, did he enter upon the work of the pulpit. He became a minister, not because he must be something, but because he could not be anything else without disobedience to God. He was to do a work for his countrymen not unlike that which Moses did for his kindred, and so, like Moses, he was called to it in the full strength of his manhood, and he entered upon it with the full persuasion that necessity was laid upon him, and woe was unto him if he preached not the Gospel. That not only made him a preacher, but it also helped very largely to make him such a preacher as he afterwards became.

Not long, however, was he permitted at this time to continue in the work which was thus begun; for in the month of July of that same year a French fleet invested the castle, whose defenders very soon surrendered, and Knox, being carried off a prisoner to France, was held for nineteen months as a galley-slave. After enduring great hardships he was liberated in the early part of 1549, when he went to England, where, under Edward the Sixth, he laboured for some years, first in Berwick, then in Newcastle, and finally as a royal chaplain, with a commission which sent him to preach in different parts of the kingdom. After the accession of Mary Tudor to the throne, however, it was no longer safe for him to remain in England; and in the end of 1553 he removed to the Continent, where, after spending some time with Calvin in Geneva, he became one of the ministers of a church of English refugees which had been formed in Frankfort-on-the-Main. But troubles with the High Church portion of the congregation, on which we cannot enter here, led him to return to Geneva, where he was chosen to be one of the pastors of the English Church that had been formed in that city. We mention these particulars because there is no doubt that the experiences through which Knox had passed in these different circumstances, and the wisdom which he had acquired through converse with some of the greatest of the Reformers both in England and on the Continent, contributed very much to the power of his ultimate ministry in Scotland. With him everything he had and learned was made to contribute to the pulpit. That was the throne of his peculiar and pre-eminent power, and the treasures of travel, as well as the accumulations of study and observation, were made to minister to his efficiency therein.

From the latter part of 1559 till his death in 1572 he continued to labour in Scotland. For the greater portion of that time he was pastor of St. Giles's Church, Edinburgh; and it may be interesting to read the record of his stated labours there, at least for the first few years. He preached twice every Sunday, and three times during the week besides. He met regularly once a week with his elders for the oversight of the flock, and attended weekly the assembly of ministers for what was called "the exercise on the Scriptures." Add to these that he was frequently appointed to perform in distant parts of the country duties akin to those of a superintendent, and we can understand how it came that his people gave him a colleague in 1563, to relieve him of some of the work by which he was oppressed.

Of his sermons only one complete specimen, printed under his own supervision, remains. He was too busy a man to write much for the press; and if he had not been called in question by the Privy Council for something in that discourse which had wounded the pride of the young Darnley, who happened to be present on the occasion of its delivery, we should not have had even that from his own pen. He tells us in the preface to it that " he considered himself rather called of God to instruct the ignorant, comfort the sorrowful, confirm the weak, and rebuke the proud by tongue and living voice, in these most corrupt times, than to compose books for the age to come ; and seeing that so much is written (and that by men of most singular condition), and yet so little well observed, he decreed to contain himself within the bounds of that vocation whereunto he felt himself specially called." But while all that is true, we have in his letters to his old parishioners in Berwick and Newcastle, and in some others of his works, sufficient hints let fall to indicate how he prepared for the pulpit; while in the statements of his contemporaries we have one or two very graphic descriptions of his manner in it.

He was a diligent student. In one of his letters he describes himself as "sitting at his books" and contemplating Matthew's Gospel by the help of "some most godly expositions, and among the rest Chrysostom." In another he writes: "This day ye know to be the day of my study and prayer to God." And in one of his interviews with Queen Mary he excuses himself from going to her privately when he had occasion to condemn her policy, by alleging that he was not appointed to go to every man in particular, and saying: "Albeit I am here now at your Grace's command, yet cannot I tell what other men shall judge of me, that at this time of day am absent from my book and waiting upon the Court." He made good use, therefore, we may be sure, of that "warm study with deals" which was constructed for him at the expense of the City Council of Edinburgh, and which is still to be seen in his house at the Netherbow.

He had a competent knowledge of Greek. Hebrew he learned after he had passed his fiftieth year, and while he sojourned in Geneva; and the mention of Chrysostom and other expositors in the quotation just given shows that he was ready and able to accept light from works which are still sealed books to many.

But the fruit of his study was never a fully written out discourse. As we learn from an incidental sentence in his "Faithful Admonition unto the Professors of God's Truth in England," it was his habit to speak from a few notes which were made on the margin of his Bible, and which remained the sole written memoranda of his discourse. He never wrote his sermons before preaching, and seldom, if ever, except on the occasions already alluded to, wrote them after. Yet they were as carefully premeditated as if they had been written, and he could apparently recall them, almost *verbatim*, for a long time afterwards. Thus we find in some of his addresses to his friends in Berwick, Newcastle, and in England generally, long quotations from discourses which had been delivered years before; and on one occasion, when he had been, as he claimed, misreported to Queen Mary, he went over the whole sermon there and then before her and the members of her Court, and his repetition was declared to be accurate by those who had heard it in the church. This indicates both that he prepared with care and that he remembered with accuracy. He did not speak extemporaneously, in the sense of never having thought upon his subject until he was required to speak; but he had fixed beforehand his line of thought, and there is reason to believe also, in many cases, the very words in which he had determined to express himself. Yet, though he premeditated very carefully, he was able also to introduce what was given to him at the moment; for when on one occasion Kirkaldy appeared in the cathedral with a retinue of armed men, as if to intimidate him, he did not hesitate to bring into the body of his sermon a very stern rebuke of that which he regarded as a serious offence on the part of one who had been a companion with him in the galleys of France.

The form of his discourses was expository. This is evident not only from that one which he printed in self-vindication, but also from the others which he has referred to and described in portions of his writings. He set himself at first calmly, clearly, and fully to explain the meaning of the passage on which he was engaged. He was particular to bring out its application to the occasion in reference to which it was employed by the sacred writer. In this portion of the discourse there was evidence of considerable scholarship, immense familiarity with Scripture, good acquaintance with ancient history, and great fervour of spirit. Having thus brought out the meaning of the passage, he then set himself to enforce its practical bearing on the circumstances of his hearers and his times, taking care first to establish the parallelism between the original case referred to by the sacred writer and that to which he applied it. This was the tip of the arrow, to which all else was but its feather; and in the shooting of that arrow he spared neither age nor sex, neither rank nor class. Wherever he saw an evil which the principle in his text condemned, he brought it to bear with all his might thereon. He recognized the explanation of the present in the old inspired record of the past; and reading Scottish history in the light of that of the Israelites, he found constant opportunity for this kind of practical application.

His expositions were frequently consecutive, and carried on through a whole book of Scripture. When the famous Parliament of 1560 was in session he was "lecturing" through the prophecies of Haggai, and had suggested thereby many powerful and pungent things bearing on the re-organization of the Scottish Church, on which the States of the Realm were then engaged. There is evidence, also, that he favoured as a general thing the practice of continuous exposition, as being fraught with profit both to preacher and hearer; for in the First Book

JOHN KNOX AS A PREACHER.

of Discipline, which was drawn up mainly by him, we have the following direction regarding the public reading of the Scriptures: "We think it most expedient that the Scriptures be read in order—that is, that some one book of the Old and the New Testament be begun, and orderly read to the end. And *the same we judge of preaching, where the minister for the most part remaineth in one place;* for this skipping and divagation from place to place, be it in reading, be it in preaching, we judge not so profitable to edify the church as the continual following of one text."

In his style he was plain, direct, homely, sometimes humorous, and always courageous. His language, however, would seem to have been purer and more free from solecisms than that of most of his contemporaries, for one of his adversaries taunts him with his "Southron tongue." But if, like Jeffrey, he had parted in any degree with his "broad Scotch," it could not be said of him, as Cockburn did of Jeffrey, that he had acquired only the "narrow English;" for he had not polished away any of his power, and he never quailed before antagonism. At a time when anonymous writings were freely circulated against him he did not flinch, but averred that from Isaiah, Jeremiah, and other inspired writers, he "had learned, plainly and boldly, to call wickedness by its own terms—a fig a fig, and a spade a spade;" thus using for the first time words which have become proverbial in the language. Occasionally, too, he brought in withering irony to bear on that to which he was opposed. His prologue to his report of his disputation with the Abbot of Crossraguel reads like a bit of a sermon on the idolatry of the Mass, and is an excellent illustration of his most trenchant manner.

Here is a specimen. He has been comparing the making of what he calls the "wafer-god" to that of the idols so sarcastically described by Isaiah in the fortieth and forty-first chapters of his prophecies, and, after speaking of the workmen engaged in both, he proceeds as follows:—"These are the artificers and workmen that travail in the making of this god. I think as many as the prophet reciteth to have travailed in making of the idols; and if the power of both shall be compared, I think they shall be found in all things equal, except that the god of bread is subject unto more dangers than were the idols of the Gentiles. Men made them; men make it. They were deaf and dumb; it cannot speak, hear, or see. Briefly, in infirmity they wholly agree; except that, as I have said, the poor god of bread is most miserable of all other idols; for according to their matter whereof they are made, they will remain without corruption for many years; but within one year that god will putrefy, and then he must be burned. They can abide the vehemency of the wind, frost, rain, or snow; but the wind will blow that god to sea, the rain or the snow will make it dough again; yea (which is most of all to be feared) that god is a prey, if he be not well kept, to rats and mice, for they will desire no better dinner than white, round gods enow. But oh, then, what becometh of Christ's natural body? By miracle it flies to heaven again, if the Papists teach truly, for how soon soever the mouse takes hold, so soon flieth Christ away and letteth her gnaw the bread. A bold and puissant mouse, but a feeble and miserable god! Yet would I ask a question, 'Whether hath the priest or the mouse greater power?' By his words it is made a god; by her teeth it ceaseth to be a god. Let them advise and answer."

These sentences remind us of Latimer; and there are many passages in his "History of the Reformation," which bubble over with humour of a similar kind; so that we may be sure that it found a way also even into his sermons; and if it did, it is not difficult to explain how "the common people heard him gladly."

The doctrinal substance of his discourses was that which we now generally associate with the name of Calvin, though he had attained to the perception and acceptance of it long before he came into personal contact with the Genevese divine. He held fast by the Deity, atonement, and mediation of the Lord Jesus Christ. Luther did not proclaim the doctrine of justification by faith more energetically than he; and in every appeal he made to his fellow-men they were sure to see that "Jesus" was "in the midst." He never put himself before his Master, or sent his hearers away thinking more of him than of his message. He seemed always to be absorbed in or carried away by his subject, and that is the explanation of the fervour of manner which characterized his delivery. Who has not read that graphic description of him in his last days by James Melville? He had been constrained to leave Edinburgh for a season, and was living, in broken health, in St. Andrews, where Melville was at the time a student. Thus he writes:—"I heard him (Knox) teach there the prophecies of Daniel that summer and the winter following. I had my pen and my little book, and took away such things as I

JOHN KNOX AS A PREACHER. 53

could comprehend. In the opening up of his text he was moderate for the space of half an hour; but when he entered on application he made me so to shiver (*Scottice*, 'grue') and tremble that I could not hold my pen to write. He was very weak. I saw him every day of his teaching go slowly and warily, with a fur of martens about his neck, a staff in the one hand, and good, godly Richard Ballantyne, his servant, holding up the other armpit (*Scottice*, 'oxter'), from the abbey to the parish kirk, and by the said Robert and another servant lifted up to the pulpit, where he behooved to lean at his first entrance, but before he had done with his sermon he was so active and vigorous that it seemed as if he would knock the pulpit in pieces (*Scottice*, 'ding the pulpit in blads') and flie out of it." *

Here, then, were all the elements of pulpit

---

* We hope none of our American readers will fall into the mistake of the Frenchman who thus ridiculously paraphrases Melville's words: "Old and broken down, and so helpless as to be hardly able to crawl along, he was raised to the pulpit by two zealous disciples, where he began his sermon with a feeble voice and slow action; but soon heating himself by the force of his passion and hatred, he bestirred himself like a madman. He broke his pulpit, and jumped into the midst of his auditors, transported by his violent declamation, and words still more violent." (See McCrie's Life, p. 264, note.)

power, so far as they are human—namely, competent scholarship, careful preparation, Scriptural exposition, Evangelical doctrine, plain speech, bold utterance, and impassioned fervour. And the effects produced attest the reality of the power. At Berwick a great transformation came over the place as the result of his two years' ministry, and his effectiveness as a preacher, both there and in Newcastle, raised him to the position of a royal chaplain. Wherever he laboured, indeed, his word was with power, and the English Ambassador at the Court of Scotland was speaking of what he had himself seen when he wrote to Cecil: "I assure you the voice of one man is able in an hour to put more life in us than six hundred trumpets continually blustering in our ears." But indeed the Reformation in Scotland was itself very largely the result of his preaching. No doubt it was begun before he entered on the work, and there were others labouring as well as he; but to him most of all are due the organization and conservation of the work in the formation of a National Church. By his ministry the entire face and future of Scotland were changed. She has made great progress in many directions since his day, and outgrown many of the limitations within which, perhaps, he would have restricted her, but the success of his work made it possible for her to become what she is to-day. And it was as a preacher mainly that he did his work. He was a statesman, indeed, as his great scheme of education clearly proves; and the fact that his advice was sought by multitudes in difficulties is an evidence that he was a man of wisdom. But though different excellencies might come out of him on different occasions, in the pulpit they were all in exercise and always at their best. That was the glass which focussed all his powers into a point, and quickened them into an intensity which kindled everything it touched. It brightened his intellect, enlivened his imagination, clarified his judgment, inflamed his courage, and gave fiery energy to his utterance. He was never elsewhere so great in any one of these particulars as he was when in the pulpit in them all; for there, over and above the fervid animation which he had in such large measure, and the glow of enthusiasm which fills the soul of the orator as he addresses an audience, he had the feeling that he was called of God to be faithful, and that lifted him entirely out of himself. He spoke because he could not but speak, and his words went *in* to men. Like those modern missiles which burst within the wounds which they have made, so his words *exploded within the hearts* of those who received them, and set them on fire with convictions that flamed forth in conduct. It was apparently impossible for any one to listen to him without being moved either to antagonism or to agreement, or—for he could be tender also—to tears.

It may be said, indeed, that he allowed himself too great liberty in commenting in the pulpit on public men and national affairs; and we may readily admit that in ordinary times and under altered circumstances it would be unwise in most preachers to do precisely as he did; but we have to bear in mind that the crisis through which his country was passing at that time was as much religious as political, and that the pulpit was the only organ at his command. To his credit be it recorded that he was, if not the first, at least among the very first, to perceive the importance of making and guiding public opinion aright. He saw that the people were to be the ultimate arbiters of the great matters that were then in debate, and he was determined to reach them. But the daily press was not then born, few, comparatively speaking, could even read, so that pamphlets were of little use, and the public meeting had not yet come into existence. Only the pulpit was his, and so, by his five sermons a week in Edinburgh,

JOHN KNOX AS A PREACHER.

and his frequent itinerancies through different parts of the country, he did what is now done by editors in their columns and by statesmen in their campaigns, and the like. He was not always wise, neither was he always discriminating, in his utterances; but he was always transparently honest, unflinchingly bold, and unselfishly patriotic; and when we add that all these qualities in him were raised to the white heat of enthusiasm, and fused into the unity of holiness by his devotion to the God and Father of our Lord Jesus Christ, we are at no loss to account for the magnitude of the work he did. He spoke and wrote and acted as ever in His sight; and more, perhaps, than any other man in modern history, he might have taken for the motto of his life the oft-repeated asseveration of Elijah, "As the Lord God of Israel liveth before whom I stand." This was the secret of his courage, the root of his inflexibility, and the source of his power.

But now, reverting to the statement with which I began, let me pause for a few moments longer to point out in what particulars especially the preaching of Knox impressed itself upon the pulpit of Scotland. It did so, pre-eminently, in these three: its expository character, its vehemence of manner, and its unflinching courage.

To his example Scotland owes the custom observed by, I believe, the majority of its ministers, down even to the present day, of devoting at least one of the discourses of the Sabbath to the regular and consecutive exposition of some book of the Scriptures. In the hands, indeed, of those who have not had the diligence to go beneath the surface, or the skill to make their work interesting, that method has often degenerated into a mere apology for preaching, consisting of the Bible and water—mostly water. But in Scotland, for the most part, it has been faithfully, laboriously, and acceptably done, and there can be no doubt that it has largely contributed to the Biblical intelligence both of ministers and people. I can remember how, in the home of my boyhood, it was my father's regular custom, on the morning of the first day of the week, to spend the time between family worship and the hour of public service in perusing a commentary on the passage which was to form the subject of exposition in the sanctuary, in order that he might be the better fitted to follow and appreciate the discourse which he expected from his pastor. A preparation that, much more wholesome than the reading of the Sunday newspaper, which, alas! has found its way into the homes of too many even of our church-members in these days.

JOHN KNOX AS A PREACHER. 59

This regular exposition of the Scriptures in all the churches made the Bible the handbook of the people. It made Scotland for long a nation of one book; and if the man who may be so characterized is proverbially dangerous, it is not wonderful that the nation of whom that was true was terribly troublesome to such rulers as it had sometimes to deal with; for the Bible and despotism cannot long live together, and it is not usually the Bible that has to go. Thus expository preaching is good for the welfare of the nation as well as for the edification of the Christian, and it were well if some American Knox, by the influence of his instructive and successful example, could bring it back to the pulpits of our land.

Not less potent on the Scottish ministry as a whole was Knox's influence in the department of manner. It is difficult, indeed, for one now, as he reads that sermon which so enraged Darnley, to understand how it could be delivered in a frenzy like that which James Melville has described. It is not nearly so strong in its language as are many other separate passages which have been preserved in other parts of his writings, and as we peruse it now it seems calm enough. But probably the manner overawed Darnley, and communicated itself to the matter, making it like red-hot shot, and putting more into the words than without it they would have conveyed. Perhaps this will account also for the fact that Knox's repetition in the palace to Queen Mary of a sermon which he had preached the previous day in the cathedral did not seem, even to her, to warrant the assertions which had been made to her concerning it by those who had heard it the day before in public, for the vehemence of the pulpit would be wanting in the parlour. But if that be, indeed, the explanation, it only shows how important the manner is; and in any case the same contrast between the calmness of the printed page and the passion of delivery which we read of in Knox reappeared in Rutherfurd and Chalmers, and repeats itself to-day in such living preachers as Cairns and Caird. But it would be wrong to regard it as a mannerism, which is either artificially acquired by the man himself or capable of imitation by another. Whatever you may call it—*præfervidum ingenium*, or whatever else—it is certainly not a mere external thing. It is as far removed from that gesticulation which an old friend of mine used to call "arm-work" as it is from "the stare and start theatric practised at the glass." It is nothing short of a "possession" of the man for the time being by the Spirit of his utterance, so that without any consciousness on his part of what he is doing it speaks through him—that is, not through his words only, but through his entire personality—and bears him along as with an overflowing flood. But, alas! with too many of us the sermon does not possess even the voice—perhaps because there is no spirit in it to become a possessor, for that is the first requisite, and where that is wanting we may say as the servant of Elijah did, when he looked so often vainly for the cloud, " There is nothing." But when a preacher is, like Knox, *sermon-possessed*, the vehemence will seem to be so natural that it will be lost sight of in the experience of the power of which it is the concomitant, and this has been true of all the best preachers in the land of Knox.

Finally, the courage of Knox seems to have been for an inspiration to all the noblest ministers of Scotland. In him the independence of the nation was sublimed, elevated, and glorified by Christian faith. Morton said of him with truth that he "never feared the face of man." But James the Sixth might have said the same of Andrew Melville; Charles the First might have repeated the words over Alexander Henderson; and Richard Cameron, whose blood reddened " the wild and lone Airdsmoss," needs nothing more than such a death to testify to his dauntless utterance of what he believed to be true. There have been, no doubt, in Scotland, as elsewhere, degenerate men, who trimmed their sails to every breeze, and always faithfully consulted their own safety and interest, but still the noble example of Knox has animated and influenced the Scottish ministry all along, and his name yet stirs the heart and quickens the pulses of a Caledonian with an enthusiasm akin to that with which he hears those of Wallace and Bruce.

I have somewhere read of a political party who wished to carry their purposes by all sorts of means, and as one of these endeavoured by corrupting the clergy to get them to support their views. This they called "*tuning the pulpits.*" But in a far nobler sense, and in a manner at once pure and lofty, Knox may be said to have "tuned" the pulpits of his nation, for he struck the key-note to which—however much, sometimes, it may have been drowned by noisy clamour, or may have seemed to become faint and almost inaudible—all that is best in the preaching of Scotland to this hour has been harmonious and true. Would God that it might be heard here among you to-day with similar effect on your life-work in this land!

III.

MELVILLE.—RUTHERFURD.—DICKSON.— LIVINGSTONE.

THE greatest names in the history of the Scottish Church between the death of Knox and the Revolution settlement were those of ANDREW MELVILLE, ALEXANDER HENDERSON, SAMUEL RUTHERFURD, and ROBERT LEIGHTON; though the last belonged to the mediating party who sought to intervene between the extreme doctrinaires on either side, and thus occupied a position different from that of all the rest. Some of the field-preachers, too, in the time of persecution deserve to be held in honourable remembrance, and must in no wise be overlooked; but in the main the history of the times, ecclesiastically considered, might be written in the biographies of those whom we have named.

With ANDREW MELVILLE we have comparatively little to do here, since his work was more that of the Educational Reformer and Ecclesiastical Statesman than of the Pulpit orator, and he was a preacher for but little more than three years. Still, as he undeniably influenced the pulpit of his country through his prelections as a theological instructor both in the University of Glasgow and in that of St. Andrews, we cannot pass him altogether by in silence. He was a younger son of a landed proprietor in Angus who perished at the battle of Pinkie while Andrew was yet a boy. After receiving what education the Academy of Montrose and the University of St. Andrews could then furnish, the lad went to Paris, where he studied for two years. Thence he removed from Poitiers, where, though then only twenty-one years of age, he was made one of the Regents of the College of St. Marceon. Here he remained for three years, and thence he removed to Geneva, where, through the recommendation of Beza, he was appointed Professor of Latin, an office which he held for five years. On his return to Scotland, in 1574, two years after the death of Knox, he was almost immediately appointed Principal of the University of Glasgow, where he inaugurated and carried out such reforms, alike in the subjects taught and the manner of the teaching, that his nephew alleges, with perhaps a little natural if not national exaggeration, that " there was no place in Europe comparable to Glasgow for good letters during these years—for a plentiful and good cheap market of all kinds of languages, arts, and sciences."*

In conjunction with the office of Principal of the University he held that of pastor of the neighbouring parish of Govan for three years, and that was the only portion of his life during which he regularly occupied a pulpit. In 1580 he was removed to St. Andrews, where he carried out the same educational improvements as he had inaugurated in Glasgow; and after having experienced in many forms the penalty of opposing King James in his darling project of fastening Episcopacy on Scotland, he was imprisoned for wellnigh four years in the Tower of London. On his liberation he went to France, where he was appointed to a chair in the Protestant College of Sedan, and where he died in 1622 at the advanced age of seventy-seven.

The Second Book of Discipline, which is still of force in the Church of Scotland, is supposed to have come mainly from his hand. He was a ripe, and for these times a rare, scholar. In general literature he had few equals, and in the composi-

---

* See McCrie's "Life of Andrew Melville," p. 33.

tion of Latin poetry he had no superior. He was the first to introduce the study of Greek into the Scottish universities, and his Hebrew Bible was his constant companion. He clearly saw and freely said that the words Πρεσβύτερος and Ἐπίσκοπος are used interchangeably in the New Testament, and in that all modern scholars will agree with him; but when he went so far as to allege the absolute *Jus Divinum* of Presbytery, in such a sense that every other form of Church government is contrary to the Word of God, few even among Presbyterians themselves will now care to follow him. Yet his influence, more perhaps than that of any other single individual, gave currency to that opinion, so that there is a measure of truth in the saying that " Knox made Scotland Protestant, but Melville made it Presbyterian." His teachings and efforts, therefore, gave intensity to the struggle between the king and those who, as every one must allow, formed the more spiritual party in the Church. He was a brave, uncompromising, heroic man, and some of his sayings at critical times in his history became watchwords to those who came after him in the conflicts of that stirring and controversial age. Like those of Luther, they were in themselves " half-battles," or rather, perhaps, to put it more strongly, "half-victories"—for those who rallied to them were on the way to success.

One or two examples may here be given. When Morton, who was then Regent of the Kingdom, indignant at something which Melville had said, remarked, in a most suggestive manner, "There will never be quietness in this country till half a dozen of you be hanged or banished from the land," Melville replied, "Tush, sir, threaten your purple minions after that manner. It is all one to me whether I rot in the air or in the ground. The earth is the Lord's; *Patria est ubicunque est bene.* I have been ready to give my life where it would not have been half so well sacrificed at the pleasure of my God. I have lived out of your country ten years as well as in it. Let God be glorified; it will not be in your power to hang in exile His truth." *

On another occasion he was sent by the General Assembly as one of a deputation to lay a certain remonstrance before the king; and when the papers were read to the assembled council, the Earl of Arran exclaimed, in a tone of indignation, "Who dares subscribe these treasonable articles?" whereupon Melville calmly answered, "We dare," and at

---

* McCrie's "Life of Andrew Melville," p. 69.

once took the pen and appended his name. Again, in 1596, when a number of the clergy were admitted to an audience with the monarch, and his Majesty had accused them of holding seditious meetings (for so he characterized the meetings of the Church for its own purposes), and of alarming the country without reason, Melville was moved to speak after this fashion : " Sir, we will always humbly reverence your Majesty in public, but since we have this occasion to be with your Majesty in private, and since you are brought in extreme danger, both of your life and crown, and along with you the country and the Church of God are like to go to wreck for not telling you the truth and giving you faithful counsel, we must discharge our duty, or else be traitors both to Christ and you. Therefore, sir, as diverse times before I have told you, so now again I must tell you, there are two kings and two kingdoms in Scotland; there is King James, the head of this Commonwealth, and there is Christ Jesus, the King of the Church, whose subject James the Sixth is, and of whose kingdom he is not a king, nor a lord, nor a head, but a member. . . . . We will yield to you your place, and give you all due obedience ; but again I say, you are not the head of the Church ; you cannot give us that eternal life

MELVILLE.

which we seek for even in this world, and you cannot deprive us of it. Permit us then freely to meet in the name of Christ, and to attend to the interests of that Church of which you are the chief member."* This has been called Hildebrandism by Dean Stanley; and even Cunningham is disposed to look at it in that light. To my view, however, what Melville argued for was not the subjection of the State to the Church, but the autonomy of the Church in the State.

I should not be disposed to stand sponsor for all Melville's opinions, but in this scene and those others of which I have spoken he seems to me to take his place with Luther, Latimer, and other witnesses for liberty of conscience, and for the spiritual independence of the Church of Christ, which is "the freest society in the world." The spirit of Knox lived over again in Melville. He knew no fear. Opposition only stimulated him to his fullest strength. It whetted his speech and gave edge to his temper: though there was genius and something more in the reply which he gave to one who blamed him for being too fiery, when he

---

* McCrie's " Sketches of Scottish Church History," vol. i. p. 125.

said, "If you see my fire go downward, set your foot on it and put it out; but if it go upward, let it go to its own place."* Such a man would be sure to make deep and indelible impressions on his students. His positivism would be to many in the place of personal conviction, and his enthusiasm would kindle in them all a kindred flame, so that though he was not himself, for any length of time, a preacher, he must have preached through them for years after he had been driven into exile. Even yet there come from his words sparks enough to kindle our souls into eager loyalty to Christ, and that is greatness, wherever and howsoever it may be manifested.

ALEXANDER HENDERSON, the next after Melville in the Scottish Evangelical succession, was, in the earlier part of his life, less a man of affairs than the exile of Sedan, but he was more distinctively a preacher. Born in 1583, in the county of Fife, he was educated at the University of St. Andrews, where, after his graduation, he was chosen to a professorship of Philosophy and Rhetoric, which he held about eight years. In 1612 he received from Gladstanes, Archbishop of St. Andrews, a presentation to the neighbouring parish of Leuchars. He was

---

* McCrie's "Sketches of Scottish Church History," vol. i. p. 126.

at that time a strenuous supporter of the Episcopal innovations, and his settlement was so utterly opposed to the will of the people that on the day of his ordination they had nailed up the doors of the church, and the clergy who were to take part in the ceremonies had to enter the building through one of the windows. Shortly afterwards, however, an entire change was wrought, in a way quite remarkable, upon his convictions. Hearing that one of the Evangelical ministers, Robert Bruce, of Kinnaird, who had then great reputation as a preacher, was to occupy the pulpit of a parish church not far away, he went under some sort of disguise, and seated himself in an obscure corner of the building to hear him. When the text, which happened to be, " Verily, verily, I say unto you, He that entereth not by the door into the sheepfold, but climbeth up some other way, the same is a thief and a robber," was given out, the words, so descriptive of his own settlement at Leuchars, went, as he afterwards said, "like drawn swords" into his heart. The sermon which followed was a message from God to him, and resulted not only in the alteration of his views on ecclesiastical principles, but also in his true conversion to Christ.* From this time on till

---

* See McCrie's "Sketches of Scottish Church History," *ubi supra*, vol. i. pp. 218, 219.

1637 he lived in retirement, faithfully discharging the duties of his office, and diligently prosecuting the study of theology; although even then he must have been known for his defence of what he held to be right, since one of Rutherfurd's letters, dated in the year which I have just specified, indicates that multitudes were looking to him to become their leader. Nor did they look in vain, for when the stool of Jenny Geddes ignited the match which set the land aflame, he came at once to the front. His hand drafted the additions to the old covenant of 1581, which made it into the National Covenant of 1638—a covenant the signing of which, in the Greyfriars Church and churchyard on the afternoon of a chill February day, is one of the most memorable scenes in Scottish history.

Two years later he was called from his rural retreat to the pastorate of that same Greyfriars Church, which he continued to hold until his death. He filled many important offices; was Moderator of the General Assembly more than once on critical occasions; was repeatedly sent as representative of the ministers to King Charles the First; and was perhaps the leading member of the delegation of six commissioners sent from Scotland to the Westminster Assembly of Divines. He died immediately after his return from a conference with the king at Newcastle, in 1646, and was buried in that old churchyard to which the feet of so many pilgrims are still attracted in the Scottish metropolis. At the Restoration of Charles the Second the representatives of that party whose adherents disentombed the bones of Cromwell paid Henderson the compliment of effacing the inscription from his monument; but it was renewed at the Revolution, and even if it had not been so, he had graven his name too deeply in the annals of his nation for it ever to be forgotten.

During his lifetime he published three of his sermons; and so lately as 1838 a volume of discourses and prayers, apparently taken down from his lips by some admirer, was given to the press by the discoverer of the manuscript. These are exceedingly interesting, as showing not only the order of service which was then common among the Scottish Presbyterians, but also as giving a specimen of the ordinary weekly work of this distinguished man. Some of the sermons belong to a course which he was evidently delivering on the eleventh chapter of the Epistle to the Hebrews, while there are others which as clearly formed part of a series on the Christian armour as described by

Paul in the Epistle to the Ephesians, giving thus incidental corroboration to the statement which I have already made concerning the expository character of Scottish preaching. In their framework they are strictly textual, and in their substance practical rather than doctrinal. Like all the sermons of that period, they are too largely broken up into minute subdivisions, although they do not err in that respect so grievously as those of the Puritans. They contain numerous allusions to the questions and circumstances of the times, but even when dealing with these their language, though strong, is never bitter or envenomed. They were manifestly delivered without notes, but they were just as manifestly the fruit of careful study, and they were probably fully written out beforehand, but whether they were verbally memorized there is no evidence to show. Their style is simple, sometimes almost conversational, and frequently vernacular, but in matter they are always rich in " that which is good to the use of edifying, that it may minister grace unto the hearers." The prayers are particularly noteworthy for their simplicity, directness, and comprehensiveness, and for the pleading pathos, as of a son with a father, by which they are pervaded.

But though his ordinary work was thus excellent, Henderson seems to have been the great man of his day in Scotland for special occasions. When anything was to be done which required peculiar wisdom, calmness, dignity, and power, he was sure to be selected for the purpose, and he *never* failed. His prayer at the signing of the Covenant in Greyfriars Church is characterized as " sublime," though doubtless some of the sublimity was in the occasion itself; for in a city to which sixty thousand people had flocked from all parts of the country, and in a pulpit which was surrounded by a dense crowd that overflowed into and filled the churchyard, there were already the influences out of which such prayers as that of Solomon at the Dedication of the Temple are born. They get as much from the occasion as they give to it, yet when one and another and another came forth immediately after to write their names in their own blood, and some appended the words " till death," we may not doubt that the rapt fervour of the holy supplication in which they had just been led by Henderson had much to do with their enthusiasm. His sermon at the opening of the memorable Assembly in Glasgow in 1638, though hastily prepared, is full of condensed power; and the words with which he dismissed that convocation, after it had formally demolished Episcopacy in the Scottish Church, were often afterwards remembered; for he said, with something like the sternness, and the prescience, too, of an old Hebrew prophet, "We have now cast down the walls of Jericho; let him that rebuildeth them beware of the curse of Hiel the Bethelite."

As a speaker, though Clarendon characterizes his style as "flat and insipid," he must have been exceedingly effective, since the same historian avers that the king well knew Henderson to be "the principal engine by which the whole nation was moved." In the judgment of others less prejudiced against him, his speech was "quiet, grave, and weighty, yet easy and fluent." He was a ready debater, as the records of the Westminster Assembly show; and we may well believe that he would not have been selected to make one of the addresses before the Houses of Parliament and the Assembly of Divines, when they adopted the Solemn League and Covenant, if he had not been regarded as one of the most prominent orators of his time. The following extract from the discourse he made on that occasion will give a good idea of the stately march of his words and the solid weight of his ideas. Bear in mind, as I read, that the Solemn League was directed against Popery as well as Prelacy, and that the latter was regarded as particularly odious, not only in itself, but also and especially as leading on to the former:

"Had the Pope at Rome the knowledge of what is doing this day in England, and were this Covenant written on the plaster of the wall over against him, where he sitteth Belshazzar-like in his sacrilegious pomp, it would make his heart to tremble, his countenance to change, his head and mitre to shake, his joints to loose, and all his cardinals and prelates to be astonished. The Word of God is for it, as you have been now resolved, by the testimony of a reverend assembly of so many godly, learned, and great divines. In your own sense and experience you will find that, although while you are assaulted with worldly cares and fears your thoughts may somewhat trouble you, yet at other times, when upon seeking God in private or in public, as in the evening of a well-spent Sabbath, your disposition is more spiritual, and, leaving the world behind you, you have found access unto God through Jesus Christ, then the bent of your hearts will be strongest to go through with this good work. It is a good testimony that our designs and ways are agreeable to God if we affect them most when our hearts are farthest from the world, and our temper is most spiritual and heavenly, and least carnal and earthly. As the Word of God, so the prayers of the people of God in all the reformed churches are for us and on our side. It were more terrible than an army to hear that there were any fervent supplications to God against us. Blasphemies, curses, and horrid imprecations there be, proceeding from another spirit, and that is all."

After reading that passage we are prepared for the statement of Grainger, who says of Henderson: "Learned, eloquent, and polite, and perfectly versed in the knowledge of mankind, he knew how to rouse the people to war or to negotiate a peace. Whenever he preached it was to crowded audiences, and when he pleaded or argued he was regarded with mute attention." To which I would only add that his knowledge of the Bible was equal, if not superior, to his knowledge of men. He seemed to be able to lay his hand on Scriptural illustrations just as he required them, and there is always a certain "*curiosa felicitas*" in his allusions to the characters in the Word of God, and in his quotations from it, which only absolute familiarity with it can account for. In this respect, perhaps, he is most worthy of imitation by the preachers of to-day.

SAMUEL RUTHERFURD, the next great preacher on our list, was born in Roxburghshire about the year 1600, and educated at the University of Edinburgh, which he entered in 1617, and from which he received the degree of M.A. in 1621. He held the office of Regent and instructor in Latin in the same institution for two years, and then gave himself to the study of theology. He was ordained in " Anwoth by the Solway" in 1627, and laboured there till 1636, when, having given offence to the Bishop of Galloway by his utterances in ecclesiastical matters, and by the publication of a work against Arminianism, he was removed from his parish and ordered by the authorities to confine himself within the limits of the city of Aberdeen.* There he remained for nearly two years, silenced, indeed, as a preacher, but writing those letters which, more than anything else he ever said or did, have preserved his name until

---

* A natural mistake is very commonly made in regard to this matter, from the fact that in his letters Rutherfurd so frequently speaks of his " prison," and of himself as " a prisoner," but he was never in prison, in the strict sense of that term. He was banished to the city of Aberdeen, and was restricted within its limits, much as Shimei was by Solomon in Jerusalem. He could go where he pleased within the city, but was prohibited from going beyond it, and was not allowed to exercise his ministry in any form.

this day. In February, 1638, he returned to Anwoth for a brief space, but the famous General Assembly of that year appointed him Professor of Theology in St. Andrews, to which office, as well as that of assistant pastor of the parish church of that city, he was installed in the beginning of the following year. In 1643 he was sent to London as one of the commissioners to the Westminster Assembly, whence four years afterwards he returned to St. Andrews, and there he died in 1661. We have not to do with him here as a man or as an author, but as a preacher,* yet it is scarcely possible for us to ignore the two former in the third; and when we include them we are at once startled and perplexed, for I frankly confess that no character even in that stormy time seems to me so difficult to regard as a unit as that of Rutherfurd. There were two men in him, and the two were so distinct that you could hardly call him a "strange mixture," for they did not mix. The one of them seemed to have no effect in conditioning or qualifying the other, but each was

---

* For an exhaustive list of Rutherfurd's theological works, and a most judicial estimate of their value, see "The Theology and Theologians of Scotland," chiefly of the seventeenth and eighteenth centuries, by James Walker, D.D.; The Cunningham Lectures for 1870-71, pp. 8-12.

just as unshaded by the other as if it had stood alone. His letters rank in the literature of devotion with the "Confessions" of Augustine or the "Imitation" of Thomas à Kempis. One not given to exaggeration has described them as "unsurpassed in holy rapture, breathing a spirit of such devotion as if he had been a seraph incarnate, and filled with such joyous transport as if he had been caught up into the third heaven, and his heart yet throbbed with the unearthly sensation."* There is perhaps a little too much of the luscious, and he treats the marriage of the soul to God, which seems to be the central idea of his experimental theology, with a realism like that of the Song of Solomon. But the consolatory epistles are especially delightful, and the book keeps its place to this day as one of the classics of the closet, despite, or perhaps in consequence of, its leaning to the mystical. Richard Baxter, who was far from agreeing with all Rutherfurd's opinions, said of the Letters, "Hold off the Bible, such a book the world never saw the like;" and Richard Cecil said of him, "He is one of my classics; he is a real original." But his controversial

---

* Dr. John Eadie, in Mackenzie's "Biographical Dictionary."

works are often rabid and bitter in the extreme. Dr. Grosart * has said that in them "you have, speaking generally, such assumption of personal infallibility, such fierceness of contradiction, such unmeasured vituperation, such extreme narrowness of sectarian orthodoxy, and such suspicion of all who differed from him, as is alike wonderful and sorrowful." Apparently he could not put himself into the place of another, so as to see things from his angle or understand his position; and though there may be truth in the traditional story which tells of his entertaining Archbishop Usher unawares, and hearing from his lips of the eleventh commandment,† to wit, "A new commandment give I unto you, that ye have love one toward another," he seems to have very frequently ignored his obligation to obey it. With him there was only one side to every question, and that one his own and God's, to oppose which was flat blasphemy and impiety. He could make no distinction between essentials and non-essentials; the form of Church government was in his view of as much importance as the deity of Christ; and what he judged to be right was so

---

* "Representative Nonconformists," p. 202. Alexander B. Grosart, LL.D.

† See Note on page 100 : "Rutherfurd and Usher."

infallibly right that all men were bound to conform thereto. It was such disputants as he who drew from Cromwell the, for him, mild remonstrance, "I beseech you in the bowels of Christ, think it possible that you may be mistaken;" and there is special reference to him by Milton in that scathing sonnet, in the body of which are these lines:

> "Dare ye for this adjure the civil sword
> To force our consciences that Christ set free,
> And rule us with a Classic Hierarchy
> Taught ye by mere A.S. and Rutherfurd?"

And which concludes with the stinging words,

> "New *Presbyter* is but old *Priest*, writ large."

This, then, was the Janus—the two men in one—called Samuel Rutherfurd. To borrow the illustration of Mr. Innes, "It was St. Thomas and St. Francis under one hood," and the intensity behind them made both of these the strongest of their kind.*

Such being the case, both would get into his

---

* By far the finest sketch of Rutherfurd that we have seen is that of Mr. Taylor Innes, from which we have just quoted, and which is to be found in "The Evangelical Succession," Second Series, pp. 127–172. As a piece of historical criticism and spiritual discrimination it is well-nigh unequalled.

sermons, though, except when he made some "necessary digressions for the times," as he called them, the venom of his controversial nature did not intrude. At Anwoth, to which his heart always leaped back with a peculiar affection, he was the most diligent of pastors. Men said of him there: "He seemed to be always praying, always preaching, always visiting the sick, always catechising, always writing and studying." It was his joy to preach Christ to his hearers. During his banishment to Aberdeen the silence which was imposed upon him was his heaviest cross, and some of the allusions in his letters to his pulpit and parish work are exceedingly pathetic—*e.g.*: "I am for the present thinking the sparrows and swallows that build their nests at Anwoth blessed birds;" and again: "Oh! if I might but speak to three or four herd-boys of my worthy Master, I would be satisfied to be the meanest and most obscure of all the pastors in this land, and to live in any place, in any of Christ's basest outhouses." Such was his earnestness for the good of his people that he declares "his soul was taken up, when others were sleeping, how to have Christ betrothed with a bride in that part of the land;" and that "he wrestled with the angel and prevailed, and woods and trees and meadows and hills were his witnesses that he drew on a fair match (marriage) betwixt Christ and Anweth."

In the writings of his contemporaries, and those who immediately followed them, we get some interesting glimpses of the preacher and his manner. Thus Patrick Simpson says: "He had two quick eyes, and when he walked it was observed that he held aye his face upward and heavenward. He had a strange utterance in the pulpit; a kind of *skriech* (shriek or scream) that I never heard the like of. Many times I thought he would have flown out of the pulpit when he came to speak of Jesus Christ, and he never was in his right element but when he was commending him."* An English merchant, during the Protectorate, describing some of his experience in what was probably a business tour through Scotland, said :† " I went to St. Andrews, where I heard a sweet, majestic-looking man (Blair), and he showed me the majesty of God; after him I heard a little fair man (Rutherfurd), and he showed me the loveliness of Christ; I then went to Irvine, where I heard a well-formed, proper old man, with a long beard (Dickson), and that man showed me all

---

* Quoted by McCrie in his "Sketches," vol. ii. p. 64.
† Ibid., pp. 61, 62.

my own heart." That was a very remarkable and a most accurate discrimination; so accurate that, as Wodrow says, "the whole General Assembly could not have given a better character of the three men." The ideal preacher, no doubt, should combine the three in himself; yet we may not refuse the palm to him who dwelt upon the loveliness of Christ, for *that* in the end will lead to the discovery of the other two. Now that was Rutherfurd's distinctive excellence in the pulpit. He might and did deal with other themes, but these he only possessed; this one, on the contrary, *possessed* him, and whenever he entered upon it he was carried away with it. We read that, "One day when preaching in Edinburgh, after dwelling for some time on the differences of the day, he broke out with 'Woe is unto us for these sad divisions that make us lose the fair scent of the Rose of Sharon;' and then he went on commending Christ, going over all his precious styles and titles about a quarter of an hour," upon which one of his hearers said in a loud whisper, "Ay, now you are right; hold you there."* Grosart says of his practical discourses that their one merit is "that they are full of the exceeding

---

* McCrie's "Sketches," vol. ii. p. 64.

great and precious promises and truths of the Gospel," and that " they hold forth with wistful and passionate entreaty a crucified Saviour as the one centre for weary souls in their unrest, and the one hope for the world."* But, after all, is not that the " one thing needful " in all preaching ? And it is for that especially that I would hold him up for an inspiration to you. Like him, preach the living, personal Christ, once crucified, but now risen and reigning as the Saviour and Sovereign of men. Unfold his loveliness. Proclaim His merits. Hold up Himself. Let the truth which you declare to be the truth as it is in Him. Let the faith to which you urge be faith in Him. Let the loyalty which you enforce be loyalty to Him. Let the heaven which you hold before your hearers be to be with Him, and to be like Him. " Hold you there," and let your words be such as love to Him shall inspire, then you shall not lack hearers, and shall not need to lament the absence of results. But with all this forget not the " eleventh commandment," and be sure to cultivate the grace of charity.

The two other names belonging to this period

---

* " Representative Nonconformists," pp. 199, 200.

cannot be overlooked. The first is that of DAVID DICKSON, who has been already incidentally alluded to in the report of the English merchant as the preacher "who showed him all his own heart." While Rutherfurd was prosecuting his pastoral work at Anwoth, Dickson was similarly engaged in the little Ayrshire town of Irvine, where his name is still held in loving and honourable remembrance. Born in 1583, and educated at the University of Glasgow, of which, immediately after his graduation, he became one of the regents or professors in philosophy, he was ordained at Irvine in 1618, and there he continued to exercise his ministry until, like Rutherfurd, he was banished to Aberdeenshire for his opposition to the Episcopalian innovations. Ultimately, however, he was restored to his parish, where he remained until he was made Professor of Theology, first in Glasgow and afterwards in Edinburgh. But on his refusal at the Restoration to take the oath of supremacy he was ejected from his office, and he died in 1663. He was of a poetical temperament, for it is to him we owe the modern version of the popular hymn, "O mother dear, Jerusalem," and that quality no doubt lent a charm to his discourses. But their chief attraction was their simple, earnest, evangelic teaching. Unlike those who were in the habit of exhausting both a text and their hearers by a series of twenty or thirty sermons on one passage of Scripture, he generally took three or four verses for a single discourse, saying that "God's bairns should get a good blaud" (that is, lump) "of his own bread." He compared a man's taking a text to his going to a tree and shaking its branches, so that the ripest of the fruit fell, while that which was green remained; and he did not think it wise to take from a text all at once everything which it contained.* His discourses were expository in their framework, evidently the fruit of study, characterized by great simplicity, and glowing with earnestness. As one of his biographers has said:

"An apostolic brevity and simplicity in preaching was what this good man not only cultivated in himself but cordially recommended to others, and that too, in a style which they were not likely to forget. That parade of extensive reading, therefore, which indulges itself in showing all the different meanings of the text before coming to the true one, he justly

---

* For these and other particulars concerning Dickson I am indebted to a sketch of his life prefixed to the first volume of "Select Writings of Dickson," published by the Committee of the Free Church Assembly, 1845.

condemned. 'This,' he said, 'was just like a cook bringing up a piece of meat to the table, and saying, "This is a good piece of meat, but you must not taste it," and then he brings another and says the same. The cook,' he added, 'should bring them no meat but what they are to eat.' In the same strain of honest-hearted humour he condemned the use of Latin sentences and scholastic phraseology before a simple auditory. 'It is,' he said, 'as if a cook should bring up the spit and raxes to the table; these are fit to be kept in the kitchen, to make ready the meat, but they are not to be brought to the table.'" *

The simplicity of Dickson's discourses, therefore, was not for lack of depth. It was the result of his determination to be thoroughly understood. While he was in Aberdeenshire he was, unlike Rutherfurd, permitted to preach, but he found the people there so ignorant and degraded that he had to subject himself to a laborious course of preparation so as to reach down to them in order that he might raise them up. He was wont afterwards to say that the people in the North were much worse than the people in the West—for studying one day would

---

* Memoir of Dickson, prefixed to "Select Writings of Dickson," p. xxx.

have served him at Irvine, but it required two days of studying for preaching at Turiff. Remember that, please, whenever you are tempted to think that because an audience is rude and uncultivated, you may speak to it without any great forethought, for it takes labour to be simple.

It is in connection with Dickson's ministry that we come upon what in our days would be called a great revival, which lasted for five years, and which was accompanied by singular manifestations of Divine power. It began just after his return from his banishment, when his own heart was enjoying the " afterward " of the great trial through which he had been brought, and it may be regarded as an illustration of the fact that the affliction of a pastor issues often in the spiritual profit of his people. Fleming, in his " Fulfilling of the Scriptures," speaks of that great awakening in these terms: " By the profane rabble of that time it was called 'The Stewarton sickness,' for in that parish first, but afterwards through much of that country, particularly at Irvine, under the ministry of Mr. Dickson, where it can be said (which divers ministers and Christians yet alive can witness) that for a considerable time few Sabbaths did pass without some evidently converted, or some convincing proof of the power of God accompanying his word. And truly this great spring-tide, as I may call it, of the Gospel was not of a short time, but of some years' continuance . . . . which put a marvellous lustre on these parts of the country, the same whereof brought many from other parts of the land to see its truth." * But Dickson—and to this I call your special attention—was as remarkable for his learning as for his fervour and simplicity in the pulpit. Many speak now as if, like Saul's armour on the stripling David, scholarship is a hindrance to an evangelist; but that it needs never be; and in any case it was not so in this instance; for, as we have seen, Dickson was accounted qualified to fill the chair of a Theological Professor both in Glasgow and Edinburgh, and besides he was devoted to sacred duties, for he devised and partly carried out an exposition of the Scriptures, after the fashion of the Speaker's Commentary in our own times. A writer competent to express an opinion has said regarding him : " His plan was to assign particular books to men competent for the work, and to him we owe it that we have Ferguson on the Epistles; Hutchison on the Minor Prophets, Job, and the

---

* Quoted in Hetherington's "History of the Church of Scotland," vol. i. pp. 260, 261.

Gospel of John; and Durham on the Song and the Book of Revelation. Dickson himself put his hand to the work. We have his English notes on Matthew and the Epistle to the Hebrews. His exposition of the Psalms is not unknown to Christian readers still, and besides we have from him annotations in Latin on the whole of the Epistles."* In his earlier years Rutherfurd and he were bosom friends, but after 1650 they took different sides in ecclesiastical politics, Dickson being a Royalist, or, as the name of the time was, a Resolutioner;† and Rutherfurd a rigid Protester against placing any reliance whatever on either Charles; and so he came in for some of his old friend's invective. But his refusal to take the oath of supremacy at the Restoration may be regarded as a proof that he had come to see that, with whatever narrowness and intolerance, the Protesters had been the more far-seeing of the two; and in any case he had little in him of that overbearing spirit which is so great a puzzle to us in the character of the author of the famous Letters. He preached frequently after he had become a professor, but not with the same power as before, so that Sir Hugh Campbell of Cesnock gave the following

---

* Walker's "Scottish Theologians," pp. 14, 15.
† See Note II. on p. 101: "Resolutioners and Protesters."

quaint account of the several stages of his pulpit eloquence. I tell the story for the sake of its warning to all Professors of Theology: "The Professor of Divinity at Edinburgh is truly a great man; the Professor of Divinity at Glasgow was a still greater man; but the minister at Irvine was the greatest man of all;" his greatness thus diminishing just as his distance from the pastorate increased.

But I must hasten on to the other of the two names to which I alluded. In the history of the British House of Commons we come upon a man who was nicknamed "Single-speech Hamilton," because he had made only one address in Parliament, but that one had made him famous. So we might almost call JOHN LIVINGSTONE "Single-sermon" Livingstone; not, indeed, because he had preached only one sermon, or because he was eminent for nothing else, for he had, even for those eventful times, a stirring history, and was "the most popular preacher of his time," but because his name now is virtually preserved from oblivion by the effects that followed a sermon of his at the kirk of Shotts, near Glasgow, on the Monday after a Communion Sunday in 1630. Born at Kilsyth in 1603, and educated at the University of Glasgow, he was licensed to preach in 1625; but owing to the restrictions then existing he did not obtain a parish, and in consequence went to Ireland, where he laboured for a year at Killinchy, but was then suspended for nonconformity by the Bishop of Down. A year after his sentence was reversed he entered anew upon his labours, but in 1635 he was again suspended, and no prospect of restoration appearing, he determined to go to New England; but he was driven back by storms to Ireland, and finding no opening there he returned to Scotland. For ten years subsequent to 1638 he was minister of Stranraer, and thence, in 1648, he was transferred to Ancrum; but though he was one of those who were sent to treat with Charles the Second at the Hague, he fell under the displeasure of the Government after the Restoration, and was banished from the country. He found an asylum at Rotterdam, where he spent the remainder of his days in preparing a Hebrew-Latin Bible, which, however, was never published, and where he died in 1672. He was for these times a great Oriental scholar,* knowing Hebrew and Chaldee, and something of Syriac and Arabic;

---

* See Note III. on p. 102, " Education of Dickson, Livingstone, and others."

so that, as one says, " he was such a scholar as we shall not readily fall in with in these days in the Church." *

The history of his famous sermon is worth giving, if for nothing else, at least for the illustration which it furnishes of that Providence of the Holy Spirit by which little things are made to lead up to great results.

A carriage occupied by some ladies of rank broke down near the parsonage at Shotts, and the minister, having had some slight previous acquaintance with them, invited the travellers to alight and remain under his roof until the damage was repaired. As they sat they observed that the house was in a very dilapidated state, and in return for his attentions they exerted themselves to secure the erection of a new parsonage in a better situation. After he had received this great kindness at their hands, the minister asked them how he could testify his gratitude to them, and they, being earnest evangelical Christians, requested that he would invite to assist him at his next sacramental season certain preachers whose names they furnished, and among these was Livingstone, who was then chaplain to the

---

* Walker's " Scottish Theology and Theologians," p. 21.

LIVINGSTONE.

Countess of Wigton, and only twenty-seven years old. The pastor was only too glad to give his consent, and, the news spreading abroad, an immense concourse of people assembled for the occasion. The services on the Saturday and Sunday* had been so unusually delightful that the people were unwilling to depart without holding a special thanksgiving on the Monday, and Livingstone was pressed to preach. Here is his own account of the matter:
"The night before I had been with some Christians, who spent the night in prayer and conference. When I was alone in the fields, about eight or nine of the clock in the morning, before we were to go to sermon, there came such a misgiving of spirit upon me, considering my unworthiness and weakness, and the multitude and expectation of the people, that I was consulting with myself to have stolen away somewhere and declined that day's preaching, but that I thought I durst not so far distrust God, and so wont to sermon and got good

---

* For an accurate description of the service of a Scottish communion occasion of the olden time, see "Peter's Letters to his Kinsfolk," by J. G. Lockhart, vol. iii. pp. 301-334. The abuses connected with it were satirized by Burns in the "Holy Fair," but the other side of the picture has been exquisitely delineated by Principal Shairp in "Kilmahoe, and Other Poems."

assistance about an hour and a half upon the points I had meditated on: 'Then will I sprinkle clean water upon you, and ye shall be clean: from all your filthiness, and from all your idols, will I cleanse you. A new heart also will I give you, and a new spirit will I put within you: and I will take away the stony heart out of your flesh, and I will give you a heart of flesh' (Ezek. xxxvi. 25, 26). And in the end offering to close with some words of exhortation, I was led on about an hour's time, in a strain of exhortation and warning, with such liberty and melting of heart as I never had the like in public in all my life." It was almost like another day of Pentecost. Some five hundred persons were converted through that one discourse; and as one says, " it was the sowing of a seed through Clydesdale, so that many of the most eminent Christians of that country could date either their conversion or some remarkable conformation of their case from that day." * God takes long views, and by these two revivals—one in Ayrshire and the other in Lanarkshire—he prepared a people for the terrible struggle that was to come in Scotland; for it is a remarkable

---

* Fleming "On the Fulfilment of Prophecy," quoted by Hetherington in "Church History of Scotland," vol. i. p. 262.

fact that from these two counties, within the next thirty years, came a large part of the strength of that Covenanting party, the echoes of whose worship are lingering yet in the glens and among the hills of Scotland. The Gospel, dear young brethren, is not yet effete. What it did in the seventeenth century it can do again in the nineteenth. Be it yours, therefore, to prepare yourselves, by scholarship, by study, by prayer, by deep, humble, fervent trust in the help of the Holy Spirit, to preach it in utter forgetfulness of self, and you, too, will have reason to say with Paul, "I am not ashamed of the Gospel of Christ: for it is the power of God unto salvation to every one that believeth."

NOTE I. See page 82.

Rutherfurd and Usher.

The best version which I have seen of this traditional story, differing in one or two details from that given by Dean Stanley, but agreeing in every particular with that which I heard often from my father's lips in the home of my boyhood, is that given by Andrew Thomson, D.D., in his delightful little volume on Rutherfurd, which is one of the series "Men Worth Remembering." It is to the following effect: "The devout and learned Archbishop Usher was on his way from England to his diocese of Armagh, and passing near Anwoth on a Saturday afternoon, anxious to listen to the preaching of one of whose piety and eloquence he had heard much, he assumed the disguise of a wayfaring man, or mendicant, and turning aside to Anwoth Manse, asked lodging for the night. According to the custom and law of the good pastor's house, not to be 'forgetful to entertain strangers,' he was readily received. It was the practice of Mrs. Rutherfurd, while her husband was engaged in finishing his preparations for the coming Lord's Day, to gather together her servants and the 'strangers within her gate,' for the purpose of catechizing them on some religious subject; and on this occasion the stranger in lowly garb readily joined the little circle of catechumens. Probably for the purpose of testing the knowledge of the wayfarer, Mrs. Rutherfurd asked him how many commandments there were? To which he answered, 'Eleven.' Regarding this as evidence of unusual ignorance, she expressed to her husband, at a later period in the evening, her fears that the stranger was very ill-instructed in religion, and mentioned as evidence of the fact that he did not even know the number

NOTES.

of the commandments. Rising early on the Sabbath morning, and retiring for prolonged devotion to his sanctuary not far off among the trees, Rutherfurd was astonished to find that there was one there already engaged in solitary worship. It was the stranger who had been welcomed the night before to his hospitality. Listening, he was struck with the evidence which his words afforded of the religious knowledge and the depth of devotion of the suppliant; and as soon as the prayer was ended he accosted him, and told him that he was certain that he was not the mendicant that he appeared to be. Disguise was no longer necessary or possible, and Usher, not unwillingly, revealed himself. The scene ended in Rutherfurd's urging him to preach for him, to which Usher assented, not averse to conform for the day to the simpler forms of Presbyterian worship. He read out as his text those words of the Master: 'A new commandment I give unto you, that ye love one another.' This explained all. 'There,' whispered Rutherfurd to his wife, 'is the eleventh commandment.'"

NOTE II. See page 93.

Resolutioners and Protesters.

"The Resolutioners and Protesters were two parties formed in the Church of Scotland in consequence of certain resolutions agreed upon by the Commission of the General Assembly, and afterwards approved of by the Assembly itself, with respect to the admission into places of power and trust in the Army and State of such as had by various Acts of Parliament been excluded on account of their malignancy or opposition to the covenant and liberties of the nation, provided they gave satisfaction to the Church. Those who approved of these resolutions were called 'Resolutioners;' those who were opposed to them were called 'Anti-Resolutioners,' or 'Protesters,' from their having given in or adhered to a protestation against the lawfulness of the Assembly held July, 1651, at St. Andrews, and adjourned to Dundee, by which these resolutions were ratified. The protestation was given in by the famous Samuel Rutherfurd, and signed by twenty-two members. Future events showed the impolicy of these resolutions. The men who were admitted by them into places of power and trust in the Army and State became, as the Protesters always predicted, the persecutors of the Church. Had the counsels of the Protesters prevailed, the twenty-eight years' persecution might not have existed."—*Note by Rev. James Anderson in the Martyrs of the Bass, in " The Bass Rock,"* p. 181.

NOTE III. See page 95.

Education of Dickson, Livingstone, and Others.

"To explain the high attainments in learning which Dickson and his illustrious comtemporaries possessed, it may be necessary to advert to the Scottish education of this period, more especially as it is frequently misunderstood and grossly misrepresented. Andrew Melville had returned from the Continent, not only richly furnished with all the learning of the age, but with a complete acquaintance with the most effectual methods of imparting it; and such was the admirable system which he had organized for the universities of Glasgow and St. Andrews that in literary reputation they were inferior to no colleges in Europe. The *curriculum* of education for the ministry especially was such as might justly put to the blush the superficial acquirements of their modern representatives. The young pupil at his admission was expected to be a thorough proficient in Latin, otherwise he could not understand the prelections, which were generally delivered in that tongue. In addition to the higher

Latin classics with which the course commenced, the students were initiated into the Greek Grammar, and carried through the ample routine of the Greek poets and historians. To these literary acquirements succeeded the study of rhetoric, ethics, physics, geometry, and history; after which the *alumni* were introduced to their more important work of studying theology as a science, in all its departments, and the Eastern languages with which it is connected. This course continued for six years, and without those long vacations which have crept into modern education. This rigid training was by no means terminated with a six years' course in the case of the most eminent of our Scottish divines. Such as had most highly distinguished themselves by talents and acquirements during that period were appointed professors, or regents, as they were then called, and in this capacity they had ample opportunities of maturing what they had already learned, as well as of enlarging the bounds of their knowledge, and after regenting for eight years they were then admitted into the ministry."—*Life of David Dickson, prefixed to " Select Writings of Dickson,* pp. vi. vii." *Published* 1845 *by the Committee of the Free Church Assembly.*

IV.

ARCHBISHOP LEIGHTON.—THE FIELD PREACHERS.

BEFORE entering upon the special period to be covered by the present lecture, we must pause a moment or two for the purpose of taking in the historical situation. After the union of the crowns of England and Scotland it seems to have been one great object of the ambition of the Stuarts to assimilate or unite the churches of the two kingdoms by fastening Episcopacy upon Scotland. This they all sought to accomplish by the mere force of civil authority, irrespective altogether of the preferences of the people. Thus resistance to their dictation became a struggle for civil freedom as well as, and indeed ultimately perhaps fully more than, a dispute about ecclesiastical government; and although the Covenanters themselves would have been glad enough to have effected a union of the churches by making England Presbyterian, and even sought to accomplish that end by force of law through the Solemn League and Covenant, yet their efforts and sufferings in opposition to their oppressors contributed to the securing of a larger liberty than they themselves would have approved. "They builded wiser than they knew," and in the evolution of God's providence they are seen to be among the pioneers of civil and religious freedom. The design of the Stuarts was largely checkmated in the case of James the Sixth of Scotland and First of England by the Scottish Parliament of 1792; and in that of Charles the First by the Edinburgh riot in 1637; the signing of the National Covenant in 1638; the famous General Assembly which met in Glasgow in the same year; the signing of the Solemn League and Covenant in London in 1643; the execution of Charles himself in 1649; and the benevolent despotism of Cromwell during the Protectorate. But with the restoration of Charles the Second to the throne of his ancestors a reign of terror was inaugurated which has its parallel only in the cruelties of Alva in the Low Countries and the deeds of the Dragonnades in France.

In December, 1661, four Scottish ministers—James Sharpe, afterwards so foully murdered on Magus Moor, James Hamilton, Andrew Fairfowl, and ROBERT LEIGHTON—were ordained in London as

priests, and consecrated as bishops to the dioceses of
St. Andrews, Galloway, Glasgow, and Dunblane respectively, in order, if possible, to carry out the
royal programme. They started to go down with
great state in a new carriage to Edinburgh, intending to make a formal entry into the northern
capital; but Leighton, already disgusted with his
companions, left them at Morpeth to carry out
their intention by themselves, and made his way
quietly to the house of a friend, near his former
parsonage of Newbattle.

Shortly after this, when the Earl of Middleton
came down to Scotland as the king's commissioner,
Fairfowl, the Archbishop of Glasgow, complained to
him that none of the younger ministers of his
diocese who had entered office since 1649 had
attended his ecclesiastical courts or would recognize
his episcopal authority, and suggested that an ordinance should be made to the effect that unless
within a given date all who had begun their
ministry subsequent to 1649 should obtain presentations to their parishes, and should apply to the
bishops for collation and admission, they should be
ejected from their homes, their pulpits, and their
livings. Judging others probably from himself, he
supposed that in the face of such a penalty all but

a very few would conform; and in an evil hour the Council, most of whose members were said to have been at the time intoxicated, passed that drastic measure which afterwards became infamous as the Glasgow Act. Only one month's warning was given, and soldiers were commanded to pull the preachers from their pulpits if they should venture to disobey. The result was that on the last Sabbath of October in that year (1662) two hundred pastors took farewell of their flocks, and soon after nearly two hundred more followed their example, thus anticipating by almost two hundred years the memorable disruption of 1843, but with this difference, that the Covenanters acted singly, each one for himself, while the Free Church men were sustained by mutual counsel, and had taken measures for their future organization. These four hundred were the "outed ministers" of whom we read so much in the histories of the period; and their noble self-sacrifice as they went forth from their manses, not knowing whither they went, but casting themselves upon Him whom they were seeking to serve, was one of the sublimest offerings ever laid upon the altar of conscience. Not quite two months before, on St. Bartholomew's Day, their act had been paralleled in England, when two thousand clergymen had left their parsonages and parishes rather than conform to the Act of Uniformity which had been enforced there; and so within two years after his restoration to the throne this was Charles's commentary on the solemn declaration which he had made at Breda to the following effect: "We do declare a liberty to tender consciences, and that no man shall be disquieted or called in question for differences of opinion in matters of religion which do not disturb the peace of the kingdom, and that we shall be ready to consent to such an Act of Parliament as upon mature deliberation shall be offered to us for the granting of that indulgence." But then the Stuarts, like the Cretians, were "always liars," and these and similar doings of theirs give point to the witty epigram written as an epitaph for one of them :

"Here lies our sovereign lord the king, whose word no man relies on,
Who never said a foolish thing, and never did a wise one."

After these four hundred ministers had been thus "outed" from their parishes, curates whom even Bishop Burnet describes as taken from "the dregs and refuse of the northern parts" were put into their places, so that the people did not care to wait upon their ministry, and sought the services of their old pastors in conventicles which assembled in retired spots on the moors or among the hills, with no roof above them but the sky. More than once, as at Rullion Green, Drumclog, and Bothwell Bridge, they defended themselves by an appeal to arms, and the persecution to which they were subjected, and in the course of which eighteen thousand people were in one way or other put to death, lasted, with occasional lulls, more or less brief, throughout the reigns of Charles the Second and James the Second, and was terminated only by the Revolution, which placed William of Orange on the British throne.

For the revolting details I must refer you to the numerous monographs on the Scottish Covenanters,*

---

* The most reliable summaries of the history of the Covenanters are such works as the following: "The Scots Worthies," by John Howie, of Lochgoin—best edition that edited by Rev. W. H. Carslaw. Edinburgh: Johnson, Hunter & Co., 1870; "The Martyrs and Heroes of the Scottish Covenant," by George Gilfillan. Edinburgh: Gall & Inglis; "Fifty Years' Struggle of the Scottish Covenanters," by J. Dodds. Edinburgh: Oliphant & Co.; "The Scottish Covenanters," by James Taylor, D.D. London: Cassell; "The Wigtown Martyrs," by Rev. Alexander Stewart; the valuable volumes of the late Dr. Simpson, of Sanquhar, entitled "Traditions of the Covenanters;" and "A Voice from the Desert; or, The Church in the Wilderness."

but I have said enough to give you an intelligent idea of the situation when Leighton entered upon the bishopric of Dunblane. That a man like him should be found on the side of those who were driving things to such extremities is as remarkable as it is that, having taken that position, his memory should now be regarded, even by Scotchmen generally, with a veneration akin to that which they cherish for the martyrs to the cause to which he was opposed. One can understand how Charles came to press him into such a service, for his character for saintliness was even then well known; and just as Jehu sought to give respectability to his unscrupulous deeds by getting Jehonadab the Rechabite to ride with him in his chariot, so we may well believe that Charles was glad to get some man of worth identified with his enterprise. But it is more difficult to account for Leighton's acceptance of such a position. One thing, at least, is clear. He had no hereditary reasons for being partial to the Prelatic party, for his father had his ears cropped and his nose slit, and was condemned to stand in the pillory, and to be put into prison, for having published a work entitled "Zion's Plea against the Prelates." It was not a very temperate book, for it had in it not a little of the bitterness which was characteristic of the controversies of the period, and from which not even Milton can be said to have been altogether free; but it had nothing whatever in it that could be a justification of such cruel treatment.

Robert Leighton was born, probably, in London, in 1611, and at the age of sixteen he was sent down to Edinburgh University for his education, just about the time at which his father was subjected to the ignominy of the pillory. After finishing his student course he spent ten years on the Continent, where he came into close fellowship with some of the Jansenists, from whom it is conjectured that he received those leanings in the direction of quietism which marked his life. He returned to Scotland in 1641 —the year of his father's release from prison—and after receiving licence to preach he was ordained as a Presbyterian minister at Newbattle, where he remained till 1653, when he was appointed Principal of the University of Edinburgh. He held that position for eight years, and was then consecrated Bishop of Dunblane.

Up till that time he had been a Presbyterian, but though he had signed the covenant with his people in 1643, there is evidence that during the latter part of his pastorate at Newbattle he was be-

ginning to find himself out of sympathy with the
Divine right doctrines of his co-presbyters, and was
glad to find a retreat in the University. He did
not believe that any form of Church government
was laid down in Scripture, and he was indeed
largely indifferent to the whole matter of ecclesiastical polity, so that he might have said, " that which
is best administered is best." Therefore he sacrificed no principle in accepting a bishopric, and yet
he was never perfectly happy in his position as a
bishop. He had really nothing in common in the
highest parts of his nature with the Sharpes and
the Fairfowls, with whom he was officially associated.
He hated the intolerance which they manifested,
and was so utterly opposed to the cruelties which
they practised that he went so far as to complain
of them to the king, and declared that " he could
not concur in the planting of the Christian religion
itself in a country in such a violent manner, much
less a form of Church government." *

---

* This is the opinion even of Episcopalians now. Lieutenant-Colonel Alexander Ferguson, in his interesting
monograph on " The Laird of Lag," has said that " no fair-minded and intelligent Episcopalian can read the history of
the period of restored Episcopacy under Charles the Second
and James the Seventh without a sense of shame and
humiliation. ' It isn't for men to make channels for God's

Even as early as 1665 he desired to resign his office, but he allowed himself to be overpersuaded again, and after labouring ten years in Dunblane he was made Archbishop of Glasgow, but finally, in 1674, he gave up his charge, and retired to the home of his sister in Broadhurst, Sussex, where he lived in privacy for ten years more, and died, strangely enough, according to a wish of his own, in an inn, on the 25th of June, 1684.

He was apparently a man "born out of due time." He had something of the ascetic, and something also of the mystic in his nature. He sought to live above the "mad whirl" and "dim confusion" of the world, and was ever a lover of peace. With very definite views of his own both in theology and other matters he did not care to fight for their supremacy, and was much of the same mind as he who said, "I had as lief be a martyr for love's sake as for truth's." He had not the qualities needed to fit him to be a leader even in the best of times, much less in that seething and tempestuous age into the

---

spirit as they make channels for watercourses, and say, "Flow here, but flow not there,"' quoth Dinah Morris, and it is true. But at the period in question the current of common justice was held back, civil liberty was lost."—*The Laird of Lag: A Life-sketch*, p. xv.

midst of which he was sent. The temptation which allured him to consent to become a bishop was the hope that thereby he might act as a mediator between the two contending parties, with neither of whom, owing perhaps to his long absence from Scotland in his early manhood, was he in full sympathy. He honestly attempted to construct a platform on which both might stand, and he conducted the affairs of his diocese in a way that was studiously conciliatory, while he held himself aloof from all the cruelties which were committed by Sharpe and others in the name of loyalty and religion. But in all this he pleased neither party. By the Presbyterians he was regarded as a traitor, and by the Episcopalians he was treated as a trimmer. But the fineness of his spirit and the thoroughly Evangelical character of his works have redeemed his name from the reproach which contemporary combatants had cast upon it; and now that the smoke and din of the battle have passed away, his influence as a preacher is felt by ministers of all denominations more than that of any man of his generation. Indeed his name marks the beginning of a new era in the history of the Scottish Pulpit. Not that he made anything like a new doctrinal departure, for he was a sincere Calvinist.

Coleridge, indeed, tries to make it appear that he was a Calvinist only in some private sense of his own; but it is impossible to read his Exposition of 1st Peter without coming frequently into contact with the doctrines that are usually identified with that system. He held, as Blaikie* says, "that the ultimate authority and supreme judge of truth for man is God, speaking to him in the Scriptures, and that the simple fact that God has there proclaimed it ought to secure for any doctrine the unqualified acceptance of all men." So far he was like his predecessors, but he held also "that to secure for truth its fitting place and its due influence in the soul, it is desirable to remove prejudices, to appeal to whatever in the soul comes nearest to it, to establish for it a friendly relation to something which is there already, and thus to get it to move sweetly and freely among the springs and motives of our being"†— and therein he was in advance of all who came before him. He abode by the old truths, but he put them in an attractive form, and brought all the resources of a great learning, all the treasures of a fine fancy, all the unction of a devout heart, and all

---

* "The Evangelical Succession," Second Series, p. 204.
† Ibid.

the beauty of an occasionally exquisite style, to bear on their illustration and enforcement.

He is the one Scottish preacher of that time whose discourses can be read not only without difficulty, but even with enjoyment by the modern student. There is more or less of uncouthness in the language of all with whom, up till this point, we have been dealing. Their dialect, if so we may call it, was a decoction of Latin, which was the language of the universities; English, which was the language of the press; and Scotch, which was the language of conversation.* Therefore they cannot now be intelligently read by any of you without a glossary. But Leighton was so far beyond his own age in this respect that he is little behind ours. He has, indeed, now to us here and there a flavour of the antique, but, so far from taking away from the interest with which we read him, that only adds to the effect which he produces, just as a slight foreign accent frequently gives increased fascination to a speaker. But perhaps the most striking feature of Leighton's discourses is to be found in the beauty and appositeness of his illustrations. In this respect he is far ahead of the

---

* Blaikie, "The Evangelical Succession," Second Series, p. 207.

preachers of his own times, and not surpassed by many of any time. He brought his similes from the wide domain of his reading, or from the realm of nature, or from the sphere of common life, with a profusion that indicates the wealth of his resources, and with a point that never leaves us in doubt as to that which he meant to illustrate by them. He did not go off away from his subject altogether like Jeremy Taylor, with a "So have I seen," and then come back after a long digression to the matter which had been wellnigh overlaid by his description. But when he used a simile, it did its work in a moment, like a flash of summer lightning in the stillness of the night; and when he employed a prolonged metaphor, he never lost himself or befogged his hearers by mixing incongruities. As an example of the first, take this clause concerning the necessity of composing our minds to due thoughts of God before entering on prayer: "This would do much to ballast our minds, that they tumble not to and fro, as is their custom;" or this, which has become hackneyed now, but was probably used for the first time by Leighton: "These divine truths are like a well-drawn picture (portrait), which looks particularly upon every one of the great multitude that look upon it." As an instance of the second, take this exquisite passage concerning the Old Testament prophecies: "This sweet stream of their doctrine did as the rivers, make its own banks fertile and pleasant as it ran by, and flowed still forward to after-ages, and by the confluence of more such prophecies grew greater as it went, till it fell in with the main current of the Gospel in the New Testament, both acted and preached by the great Prophet Himself, whom they foretold to come, and recorded by His apostles and evangelists, and, thus united into one river clear as crystal, this doctrine of salvation in the Scriptures hath still refreshed the city of God, His Church under the Gospel, and still shall do so, till it empty itself into the ocean of eternity." All his writings belong, as his latest editor has clearly made out, to the Presbyterian portion of his life, and they are evidence that he made very careful written preparation for his pulpit. Whether he committed to memory what he had written, and so gave it to the people, is uncertain. But he did not read from a manuscript, for as to that practice he said: "I know that weakness of memory is pleaded in excuse for the custom, but better minds would make better memories. Such an excuse is unworthy of a man, and much more of a father, who may want vent, indeed, in addressing his children, but ought never to want matter. Like Elihu, he should be refreshed by speaking." As to his manner, Baillie speaks of it as "the new guise of preaching which Mr. Hugh Binning and Mr. Robert Leighton begun;" and Burnet says it was "rather too fine," but adds, "there was a majesty and beauty in it that left so deep an impression that I cannot yet forget the sermons I heard him preach thirty years ago." When he left Newbattle he gave as a reason for desiring to demit the pastorate "the extreme weakness of his voice;" and there could at no time have been in it the "skriech" of Rutherfurd; while his style as written seems entirely unsuited to the vehemence that we have marked in some of his predecessors. His personal appearance is thus described by a poet-preacher who occupies to-day no mean place in the Scottish pulpit:

> "A frail, slight form—no temple he,
> Grand, for abode of Deity;
> Rather a bush inflamed with grace,
> And trembling in a desert place,
>   And unconsumed with fire,
>   Though burning high and higher.

> "A frail, slight form, and pale with care,
> And paler from the raven hair
> That, folded from a forehead free,
> Godlike of breadth and majesty—

A brow of thought supreme,
And mystic, glorious dream.

" Beautiful spirit! fallen, alas!
On times when little beauty was;
Still seeking peace amidst the strife,
Still working, weary of thy life;
    Toiling in holy love,
    Panting for heaven above.

" For none so lone on earth as he,
Whose way of thought is high and free,
Beyond the mist, beyond the cloud,
Beyond the clamour of the crowd;
    Moving where Jesus trod,
    In the lone walk with God." *

Somewhat of his own "higher life" there is in these last lines, and an undue glorification of the contemplative above the active, the devotional above the militant, in the Christian character; for if God puts a man into a crowd, he does not ask him to move above it, but to go through it. Still, the whole description puts Leighton graphically before us as he was, and with this knowledge of his environment I ask you, my young brethren, to give diligent study to his works. They will feed your piety even while they quicken all your homiletic powers. Put them in a prominent place upon your devotional

---

* "The Bishop's Walk." Walter C. Smith, D.D.

shelf, and take them often down to fill in for you those fragmentary minutes which otherwise would be lost. Ever and anon you will come upon such nuggets as these: "The Sunday's sermon lasts but an hour or two, but holiness of life is a continued sermon all the week long;" "The master's mind is often more toiled than the servant's body;" "Where there is no feeling at all there can be no patience;" "The Church is the jewel in the ring of the world." Frequently, also, as in his treatment of the doctrine of election, or his comment on Christ's bearing our sins, you will find the truth stated in a most striking and attractive manner, and with such an appreciation of the very point where the difficulty lies as enables him to do much in the way of removing it altogether. He has been for long to me one of the richest of my classics for the closet; and if you think that I have "exceeded" in my eulogy, I can only say that I have come honestly by my admiration of the good archbishop; for Dr. John Brown, of Edinburgh, at whose feet I sat when, like you, I was preparing for the ministry, was most hearty and emphatic in his praise, and has left on record the following testimony to his worth, behind which I am quite willing to shelter myself even when I adopt it as my own. Speaking of the Exposition of 1st Peter, he says: "That very remarkable work teaches a singularly pure and complete theology—a theology thoroughly evangelical, in the true sense of that often abused epithet, being equally free from Legalism on the one hand and Antinomianism on the other; in a spirit of enlightened and affectionate devotion, love to the brotherhood, and charity to all men, and in a style which, though very unequal, indicates in its general structure a familiarity with the classic models of antiquity, and in occasional expressions is in the highest degree felicitous and beautiful. As a Biblical expositor, Leighton was above his own age, and as a theologian and practical writer few have equalled, still fewer surpassed him, either before or since his time. . . . . Labouring under more than the ordinary disadvantages of posthumous publications, through the extreme slovenliness with which they, with but few exceptions, were in the first instance edited, his works are eminently fitted to form the student of theology to sound views and a right spirit, and to minister to the instruction and delight of the private Christian—possessing in large measure and rare union those qualities which must endear them to every Christian mind, however uncultured, and those which are fitted to afford high gratification to them in whom the knowledge and love of evangelical truth are connected with literary attainment and polished taste." * When I first heard these words from the lips of my revered instructor, I believed them on his testimony, but I know their truth now from my own experience, and I pass them on to you that you may profit from them as I did. It would not be good, perhaps, to read nothing but Leighton, for he lacks manliness, and would not fit us for the sterner side of Christian duty; but in an age like ours, when all is stir and bustle and push, his books furnish a first-rate alterative, and help to restore the devotional to its true place in the life of the soul.

But good as Leighton was, he did little or nothing to bring the blessing of peace to his distracted country. His plan of amalgamating Episcopacy with Presbytery proved to be nothing better than "a devout imagination;" for during most of the years of his bishopric and archbishopric, and indeed for some considerable time after his death, the adherents of the Covenant were subjected to bitter persecutions. Fines for non-attendance at

---

* Preface to "Expository Discourses on 1st Peter." John Brown, D.D.

the parish churches were extracted until the victims were utterly ruined. Soldiers were quartered upon the people in such numbers that they absolutely devoured their substance. The presence of any one at a conventicle, especially if he was a minister and had preached, was held to be enough to warrant his apprehension, and that usually issued in his imprisonment on the Bass Rock, or in Dunnottar Castle, or elsewhere, or in his banishment from the country, or in his execution on the scaffold. It is not wonderful, therefore, that those who were thus oppressed lifted the sword in their defence; but *that*, after the failure of the Pentland rising, only made matters worse for the time, and heated the fire more fiercely than ever.

In 1669 the king, who did everything apparently by his own will, and without troubling himself with any Parliament, gave liberty to the Scottish Council at its discretion to appoint the outed ministers to vacant parishes under certain limitations. Many among them, with whatever reluctance, submitted to the terms imposed, and returned to the labour which they loved; others, however, sturdily refused to go back to their parishes on the conditions prescribed, and so the Covenanters were again divided, this time into those who approved and those who disapproved of the "Indulgence," as it was called. Judged by the event, the more rigid and unbending were fully justified in the course they took, although it drew upon them a fiercer persecution than ever; but it is hard to blame with any severity the men who, weary of what seemed to be a vain resistance, allowed themselves to be allured back to their pulpits and their people, even though the terms on which they returned amounted almost to the stultification of their former heroism. Indeed, as to this whole struggle it is exceedingly difficult to get at a perfectly unbiassed estimate of the men who took part in it, and certainly I cannot pretend to rigid impartiality in the case, for one of my own direct ancestors, Captain John Paton, of Meadowhead, was a prominent leader among the laymen, and fought valiantly at Pentland and Bothwell Bridge, ultimately laying down his life on the scaffold in the Grassmarket of Edinburgh for the cause with which he was identified. But I am persuaded that the "Poundtext" of "Old Mortality" is no better a representative of the Indulged clergyman of the period than the "Kettledrummle" is of the field-preachers of these times.

In the "History of Kilmarnock" there is mention made of a Mr. Wedderburn, one of the Indulged, who is said to have been much esteemed for his worth, piety, and learning, and who drew upon himself a blow from the musket of a soldier for attempting to remonstrate with the military on their discreditable conduct in the pillaging of the people.* On the other hand, the traditional descriptions of those whose voices were so often heard on the open moorland forbid us to regard them as unlearned and ignorant mountebanks, after the type of "Mucklewrath," or half-insane fanatics, like "Ephraim Macbriar." They had all received a liberal education. Some of them belonged to the best families of the land, and the uncouthness of their speech and manners was that of their times, for which they are not now more ridiculous than their contemporaries. They had their faults, and it is not to be denied that they had not attained to such views regarding civil and religious liberty as those which are now generally accepted among ourselves; while there were, perhaps, some things about them that might by modern exquisites be made ludicrous; but there was no comedy, nor anything that can by all the efforts of genius be made to appear farcical, in their sufferings. These

---

* "History of Kilmarnock," p. 49. Archibald McKay.

were all tragic—nay, because they were endured for conscience' sake they were sublime; and even those who have no sympathy with their opinions have been compelled to do homage to the purity of their motives and the calmness of their courage.

When, however, we go in search of the eloquence which is ascribed to them as preachers, we must remember that their discourses have come down to us for the most part in fragments taken as notes by their hearers amid many difficulties, and without the aid of stenography, so that they give us but little idea of the sermons as a whole. Moreover, it is not to be forgotten that much of the eloquence that was ascribed to the preachers was really in the very remarkable circumstances under which they spoke. Their conventicles were held in places far up amid the silence of the mountains, near the sources of the Nith and the Clyde, in the uplands of Ayrshire, Dumfriesshire, and Lanarkshire, or in bleak morasses like "the wild and lone Airdsmoss." The people came together sometimes in the early morning, and sometimes amid the stillness of the night, and many of the men were armed with muskets and short swords. Sentinels were posted at points of vantage to give timely warning of the coming of the enemy, and no one of them knew but that he might be called within a few hours to seal his testimony with his blood. Occasionally the Sacraments were administered. Little children were in a very true sense " baptized for the dead " with water taken from the purling brook, and the table of the Lord was literally spread full often " in the wilderness." The sound of praise at such times was borne aloft and far upon the breeze, and it was from scenes like these that the old version of the Psalms of David in metre acquired that peculiar charm which they still have for every Scotchman, indissolubly associated as they are with the patriotism of his fathers as well as with the worship of his God. They are thus to the pious peasantry of that land very much what the " Battle Hymn of the Republic " and other stirring songs are to the people of these Northern States. Nay, they are more ; for because he knows that his fathers marched to victory at Drumclog to the music of its words, the psalm which thus begins—

> " In Judah's land God is well known :
>   His name's in Israel great.
> In Salem is His tabernacle,
>   In Zion is His seat.
> There arrows of the bow he brake,
>   The shield, the sword, the war;
> More glorious thou than hills of prey,
>   More excellent art far "—

thrills his heart with an emotion that is all the deeper because the love of country combines with the love of God to give it power.

At such gatherings, therefore, there was eloquence, and that, too, of a high order, in the mere occasion; and if to-day, in reading the reports of the sermons of the field-preachers, we fail to find a full justification of the terms in which they were described by those who listened to them, we must remember that not even the ablest stenographer could reproduce the environment out of which the discourses grew and in which they were delivered. But as I have looked carefully over them, I have been struck with the fulness of their presentation of the Gospel, and the fervour of their appeals to sinners to accept Christ and His salvation. The impression among many still is the same as that which a writer of the period has exposed regarding Cameron, when he says, "I crave leave to tell you that the common report of poor Mr. Cameron was that not only did he preach nothing but babble against Indulgence, but that he could do no other thing." But the perusal of a work like Simpson's "Voice from the Desert; or, The Church in the Wilderness," will be enough to substantiate the assertion in regard to all the preachers which the writer already quoted makes concerning Cameron, when he adds: " But by his coming hither, the reporters have lost their credit of being easily believed in the future; . . . for here he was found a man of savoury Gospel spirit, the bias of his heart lying towards the proposing of Christ, and persuading to a closing with Him." They are quaint words, but they give a true description—for the climax to which all the discourses lead is " the closing " of the individual soul " with Christ." And you can see how naturally *that* came about. For the ministers were preaching, as it were, with halters round their necks, and each of their hearers might have said with David, " There is but a step betwixt me and death." It was no time, therefore, for playing with rhetoric, or for cultivating the graces of style, or for dealing in matters of mere speculation. They came to the point at once; and while, as was to be expected, there were many references to the trials of their times and the tyranny of their oppressors, the great object of all their sermons was the presentation of Jesus Christ and Him crucified. Nothing can exceed the pathos with which they besought their hearers to be reconciled to God and to endure patiently in His cause. It is not surprising, therefore, to learn that the ten years during which a large portion of the Scottish nation met thus from Sabbath to Sabbath in the hidden recesses of the country, and in defiance of the law, were ever afterwards referred to as times of special revival. I take two specimens belonging to the latter portion of the persecuting era, but yet fairly representative of the whole. What could be more effective than such an appeal as this of CAMERON, addressed to thousands on the mountain-side, from the words, " Ye will not come unto me, that ye may have life " ?

" Ye that have been plagued with deadness, hardness of heart, and unbelief, He now requires you to give in your answer—yes or no. I take instruments before these hills and mountains around us that I have offered Him unto you this day. Angels are wondering at the offer. They stand beholding with admiration that our Lord is giving you such an offer this day. What shall I say to Him that sent me ? Shall I say, ' Lord, there are some yonder saying, ' I am content to give Christ my heart and hand, house, land, and all that I have, for His cause ?' " Look over to the Shawhead and all those hills—look at them. They are all witnesses now, and when you are dying they shall come before your face." " Here," says the reporter, " both minister and people fell into a state of calm weeping." And after a long pause, Cameron, before again proceeding, offered up a prayer for the tranquillizing influences of the Holy Spirit. Truly such scenes as these are the best attestation of eloquence, whether or not we can explain or analyze the secret of its production.

Take, again, these sentences from ALEXANDER PEDEN, which rise and fall with a plaintive chant, followed ever and anon with a recurring refrain, almost as of a chorus: " Now, sirs, what is it that has carried through the sufferers for Christ these twenty years in Scotland? It is 'the fellowship of His sufferings.' It is the filling up of His sufferings according to the ancient decree of Heaven. For my part, I seek no more if he bids me go. He bade many, from 1660 to the year of Pentland, go forth to scaffolds and gibbets for Him, and they sought no more but His commission; they went, and He carried them well through. Then, in 1666, at Pentland, He bade so many go to the fields and die for Him, and so many to scaffolds and lay down their lives for Him; they sought no more but His commission; they went, and He carried them well through. Again, in 1679, at Bothwell, He bade so many go to the fields and scaffolds and die for Him; they sought no more but His commission; they went, and He carried them well through. He bade so many go to the seas, and be meat for the fishes for Him; they sought no more but His commission; they went, and He carried them well through. And afterwards, in 1680, at Airdsmoss, He bade so many go to the fields and scaffolds for Him; they sought no more but His commission; and went, and He carried them well through. This cup of suffering hath come all the way down from Abel to this year 1682 in Scotland. Our Lord hath held this cup to all the martyrs' heads wherever He had a Church in the world, and it will go to all the lips of all the martyrs that are to suffer for Christ, even to the sounding of the last trumpet. But yet, people of God, it is only the brim that the saints taste of. Be ye patient in believing. . . . . Our noble Captain of Salvation hath vanquished these bloody persecutors in Scotland these twenty-two years, more by the patient sufferings of the saints than if He had threshed down all in a moment. The patient suffering of the saints, with their blood running, declares His glory much abroad in the world, and especially in these lands. As I came through the country, there was a poor widow whose husband fell at Bothwell. The bloody soldiers came to plunder her house, telling her they would take all she had: 'We will leave thee nothing, either to put in thee or on thee.' 'I care not,' said she; 'I shall not want so long as God is in the heavens.' That was a believer indeed."

"They went, and He carried them well through." What a sweet refrain that is! And can it be possible that we have a faint echo of this old sermon in the words put by Mrs. Cross into the mouth of Adam Bede regarding Moses: "He carried a hard business well through"? I cannot tell. But this I know, that no one who heard those oft-repeated words that day would ever be able to forget them, especially when we think of them as uttered by a man whose manner is thus described by one who was often in his congregation: "Although every act of worship that Peden was engaged in was full of divine flights and useful digressions, yet he carried along with them a divine stamp; and such was the weighty and convincing majesty that accompanied what he spoke, that it obliged the hearers both to love and fear him. I observed that every time he spoke, whether conversing, reading, praying, or preaching, between every sentence he paused a little, as if he had been hearkening what the Lord would say unto him, or listening to some secret whisper; and sometimes he would start as if he had seen some surprising sight."* There was that about him, therefore, that irresistibly suggested to men his communion with the Unseen. He spoke " as seeing Him who is invisible," and *there* was the hiding of his power while pleading with his fellow-men.

Then, in the midst of all, was evermore Jesus on the cross. To Him these preachers pointed their hearers; from Him they drew their inspiration; and out of love to Him they carried on the struggle in which they were engaged. "Ye are bought with a price, be not ye therefore the bond-servants of men: " that was the principle by which they were actuated. They sought independence from men, that they might keep themselves entirely for Christ. This was what they meant by their enforcement of "the headship of Christ"; and they contended for Christ's crown because they felt that they had been purchased on Christ's cross. We do not claim for them the highest scholarship, the profoundest thought, the most polished style, or the finest eloquence; but we do claim for them that they preached Christ most effectively, and that they drew for themselves, and exhorted all their hearers to

---

* Sergeant James Nisbet, quoted in "The Bass Rock," pp. 52, 53.

draw, their motives for their daily conduct from the cross of their Redeemer; and to all their detractors they might have said with Paul: "From henceforth let no man trouble us, for we bear in our bodies the marks of our Lord Jesus."

I have given you from a living Presbyterian poet a portrait of the good Archbishop Leighton; let me gratify myself by concluding this lecture with the description given by the Episcopalian Grahame of the Covenanters' Sabbath gatherings, in his poem on " The Sabbath " :

> " Long ere the dawn, by devious ways,
> O'er hills, through woods, o'er dreary wastes, they sought
> The upland woods, where rivers—there but brooks—
> Dispart to different seas. Fast by such brooks
> A little glen is sometimes scooped, a plat
> With greensward gray, and flowers that strangers seem
> Amid the heathery wild, that all around
> Fatigues the eye. In solitudes like these
> Thy persecuted children, Scotia, foiled
> A tyrant's and a bigot's bloody laws:
> There, leaning on his spear, ...
> The lyart veteran heard the Word of God
> By Cameron thundered or by Renwick pour'd
> In gentle stream. Then rose the song, the loud
> Acclaim of praise; the wheeling plover ceased
> Her plaint; the solitary place was glad;
> And on the distant cairn the watcher's ear
> Caught doubtfully at times the breeze-borne note.
>   But years more gloomy followed, and no more

> The assembled people dared in face of day
> To worship God, or even at the dead
> Of night, save when the wintry storm raved fierce,
> And thunder-peals compelled the men of blood
> To crouch within their dens. Then dauntlessly
> The scattered few would meet in some deep dell
> By rock o'er-canopied, to hear the voice—
> Their faithful pastor's voice. He, by the gleam
> Of sheeted lightning, op'd the sacred book,
> And words of comfort spake; over their souls
> His accents soothing came, as to her young
> The heath-fowl's plumes, when at the close of eve
> She gathers in, mournful, her brood dispersed
> By murderous sport, and o'er the remnant spreads
> Fondly her wing. Close nestling 'neath her breast,
> They, cherished, cower amid the purple blooms."

The lines have fallen unto us in pleasanter places; but as we sit under the spreading branches of the goodly tree of Liberty, it becomes us to remember that the roots thereof were nourished long ago, by the blood of these men, and of the brethren and companions of these men, of whom we have been speaking. "With a great price" they purchased this liberty that we might be "free-born." Let us therefore "stand fast in the liberty wherewith," through them, "Christ has made us free."

V.

THE MODERATES AND EVANGELICALS.

DURING the eighteenth century a marked change came over the Scottish Pulpit. That was the period generally described as the Reign of the Moderates, concerning whom opinions will differ, according to the point of view from which they are contemplated. If, for example, with Dean Stanley we occupy the position of Broad Churchism, we will regard them as the advanced spirits of their age, seeking that comprehension of all creeds and classes in an Established Church which was the ecclesiastical ideal of that accomplished author. But if we have any love for definite theological teaching on such subjects as the Fall of Man and the Atonement of Christ, or anything like what seem to me to be Scriptural views of the importance of Regeneration and Conversion, we will look upon the age of their ascendancy as one of dark and disastrous eclipse.

The name by which they are popularly denomi-

nated was not one of reproach, given to them by
their antagonists, but was assumed and gloried in
by themselves; so that we are guilty of no mere
appeal to prejudice against them when we employ
the term. We have already seen that at and after
the Revolution settlement the Church of Scotland,
so far as the ministry was concerned, consisted of a
strange agglomeration of heterogeneous ingredients.
The sixty survivors of those four hundred ministers
who had been "outed" in 1662, though they
formed the nucleus of the reorganization, were in
reality, after a few years, only a small minority of
the whole. The majority was made up of those
who, having held cures during the years of Episcopacy, retained them through conforming to Presbyterianism, and who were ready to submit
to patronage enactments, and everything else,
rather than give up their livings. These last
were men of no education, little versed in doctrinal
matters, and in some instances knowing nothing of,
and caring less than nothing for, the great principles
which were so dear to the Covenanters. The
consequence was that they were averse to everything distinctively evangelical. They had nothing
but rebuke for those who were concerned in the
republication and annotation of a book entitled

"The Marrow of Modern Divinity," which, with some extravagance of statement here and there, put in the centre of its teaching the fact that God had made a gift of His Son Jesus Christ for salvation to mankind sinners as such; and they deposed the fathers of the Secession for their repudiation of Patronage. But they tolerated for years the Socinian teachings of Simpson, who was Professor of Theology in Glasgow, and at length deprived him of his chair only when his own imprudent publication of his opinions rendered it impossible for them with decency to retain him. This does not look much like comprehension, but it is only another illustration of the fact which history has often attested—that the intolerance of so-called Liberals is frequently the worst form of tyranny.

With this hatred of evangelical truth—I speak of the party, not of individuals—there was ultimately combined a devotion to the graces of style and rhetoric which was no doubt largely due to the law of reaction. In the preaching of the latter half of the seventeenth century little attention had been paid to literary matters. As Rainy has said: "Culture, development of literature, development of taste, deliberate adaptation of means to ends, had been wofully checked and marred. The peaceful processes by which those who teach and those who learn find out one another's meaning, the processes by which mind in each generation is laid under contribution for new and various services, had been sadly interrupted. . . . . A man who preached *as* he could and *when* he could, in a house or on a hillside, was not likely to take much care of his style. And the habit of the pulpit had retained in point of fact much of the old dialect and much of the old way of dividing and arranging topics, [and] it did so at a time when in general literature the most rapid improvement was taking place in these very particulars, an improvement which that age was rather disposed to over-value." *

Now, the Moderate party, as a party, gave itself assiduously to the cultivation of these literary graces, and much good would have come out of that if only it had been subordinated to the higher end of the proclamation of the Gospel. But the misfortune was that the Moderates put the means into the place of the end, so that in their hands the sermon became a mere literary product rather than an instrument for the conversion and edification of souls. No more striking exemplification of the sad influence

---

* "Three Lectures on the Church of Scotland," p. 77. Robert Rainy, D.D., in reply to Dean Stanley.

which such a practice must have upon the efficiency of the pulpit can be found anywhere than in the history of the Scottish Moderates. First, there was made by them a modification of Christianity, so as to harmonize it with culture; then there was developed a tendency to dwell rather on those things which are common to it with natural religion than on such things as are and always have been " a stumbling-block" to "the Jew" and "foolishness" to "the Greek." This was followed by a merely moral teaching, in which all doctrine was ignored, and dissertations on the virtues took the place of expositions of the Scriptures, and that in its turn was succeeded in some quarters by something that was little more than the baldest Deism. The same development was seen, unless I have misunderstood all that I have read upon the subject, in New England, at the time of the Unitarian defection, and the two histories together utter a loud warning, which I trust you young men will heed, against allowing the secondary to usurp the place of the primary, and cultivating literature or scholarship to the neglect of that for the attainment of which alone in the pulpit these things are of any value. " *The body is more than raiment.*" The raiment, indeed, in its own place is not to be despised, and the costume of a well-dressed gentleman is better by far than the blanket of the Indian; but as a covering for the dead, neither is of any great consequence, for it is only the living body that gives importance to the raiment. So cultivate style, the style of your own times, the best style of your own times, for there is no need of adhering in that matter to any Quaker-like, stereotypic anachronism; but see to it that the style clothes the living truth, and is meant not only for the expression, but also for the protection of that truth, else the result will be as disastrous with you as it was in Scotland. For the preaching of virtue, alas! did not make men virtuous, and those vices which are said to be most common among the lower orders of the Scottish people became more prevalent than ever under such instructors.[*]

Of the Moderates as preachers, the only man whose sermons have come down to us with any great prestige is Dr. HUGH BLAIR. He was the great-grandson of that Robert Blair of St. Andrews whom the English merchant described as having shown him "the majesty of God," and the son of

---

[*] See "The Scottish Philosophy," p. 19. James McCosh, D.D., LL.D.

MODERATES AND EVANGELICALS. 145

an Edinburgh citizen. Born in 1718, he was educated at the university of his native city, and was licensed as a preacher in 1741. Within a year after that he was ordained to the charge of Colessie, in Fife; thence, in 1743, he was translated to Edinburgh, where he laboured first in the Canongate, then in Lady Yester's, and finally in the High Church, until his death in 1800, at the age of eighty-two. He was distinguished in his literary course for an essay "On the Beautiful," and at the taking of his master's degree for a thesis, " De fundamentis et obligatione legis naturæ," which his biographer says, with great *naïveté*, "exhibits in elegant Latin an outline of the moral principles which have since been more fully unfolded and illustrated in his sermons."* During the early years of his pastorate of the High Church he prepared and delivered a course of lectures on Rhetoric and Belles-lettres in the university, and he was subsequently appointed as professor of these subjects to a chair which was founded and endowed for him by the Crown. It is evident from these facts that he had addicted himself, if not to literary pursuits, at least to the pursuit of literature, and that he belonged to

---

* James Finlayson, D.D., in sketch prefixed to the "People's Edition" of Blair's Sermons, p. xii.

that coterie of which the historian Robertson was the head, and which had the merit of originating and promoting that Renaissance, as I may call it, of elegance and taste which made the Edinburgh of that age so remarkable.*

Of his sermons, which were originally published in five volumes, it may be said that they were unduly praised at the time of their appearance, and that they are as unduly neglected now. Samuel Johnson called them "auro magis aurei;" and King George the Third, who was a great patron of Blair, and who gave him a pension of two hundred pounds a year, is reported to have often said that he wished to hear that the Bible and Blair's sermons were in the hands of every youth in the United Kingdom. These opinions from the leader of literature and the leader of fashion may perhaps account in some degree for the number of editions through which Blair's sermons passed; while the fact that the distinctive features of the Gospel are largely absent from them may explain the oblivion into which now they have fallen. But for style and method they may still be studied with advantage, though they do not now, of course, hold the

* See note on page 181, "The Literary Eminence of the Moderates."

same relatively high place in these respects which they did at the date of their publication. They have a distinctively modern cast, and his mode of opening up and dividing a subject is often felicitous and suggestive. In matter, however, they are exceedingly defective. One is prepared to find that this will be the case from the very terms employed by the Editor of the People's Edition in his preface, to this effect: " They treat of life and death, hell and judgment; of the superintendence of an overruling Providence, who directs and governs all the affairs of this life; of the certainty of the rewards which await the just who fulfil the precepts and obey the laws of their Creator and Redeemer; and the tremendous punishment which the wicked will suffer in another world who break His commandments and despise His statutes in this life."

This is a fair representation of the contents of the volumes, and, as you perceive, these are all doctrines of merely natural religion; for there is in the enumeration no allusion whatever to the Cross of Christ, and the truths that either centre in or radiate from that. But it would be unjust to say that Blair did not believe in the Atonement, or that he absolutely never preached about it. Out of the ninety-one sermons which he printed, six were preached on occasion of the administration of the Lord's Supper, and in at least three or four of these we have such distinct and unqualified statements of the expiatory nature of the death of Christ as no Socinian could have made. But there is little allusion to that subject in the rest of the discourses. They treat of religion, virtue, piety, vice, &c., as abstractions; and we have dissertations on "The Disorder of the Passions," on "The Importance of Order in Conduct," on "Candour," on "The Love of Praise," on "Envy," on "Friendship," and the like. But we have not a word on Repentance, Regeneration, or Faith; and, so far as I have discovered from a somewhat careful examination, there is no allusion to the existence or agency of the Holy Spirit in the whole five volumes. It would not be fair to say that he did not hold the doctrine of the Atonement, but judging from his published sermons he certainly did not put it in the place which it occupies in the New Testament, and he did not hold it as Paul held it. His sermons were, for the most part, moral disquisitions without the background of the Cross, and all the beauty of style to which a man can attain will not make amends for the absence of that; while, again, the absolute ignoring of the Holy Spirit must have deprived his utterances of power, for Keble has written no truer lines than these:

> "The spirit must still the darkling deep,
>   The dove must light upon the cross,
> Else we should all sin on or sleep
>   With Christ in view—turning our gain to loss."

And if that be the case, even "with Christ in view," it must be so, *à fortiori*, when He is studiously kept out of sight.

I remember hearing a shrewd Scotchman describe a minister of the Blair stamp as "a very innocent preacher," meaning thereby that he would do no great damage to Satan's kingdom in the world, and that was true; but as far as the kingdom of Christ is concerned, we can predicate no such innocence of those who preach discourses of this type, for they lull souls into false security, and they prepare the way for still wider defection from the truth by others. And both of these effects were undeniably produced by Blair and his associates; for by-and-by the people lost their relish for the Gospel in its purity, and called its preachers "high-flyers," "enthusiasts," "zealots," and the like, because they asserted the depravity of the heart, and said to their hearers, as Jesus said to Nicodemus, "Ye must be born again." Nor was this all, for others began where Blair left off, and things must have come to a poor pass when David Hume could say to his friend Alexander Carlyle, the minister of Inveresk, after hearing him preach a sermon in the pulpit of John Home, the author of the tragedy of "Douglas," "What did you mean by treating John's people to-day to one of Cicero's Academics? I did not think such heathen morality could have passed in East Lothian." It was bad enough when such a charge could be brought with truth against a preacher of the Gospel by any man; it was worse that David Hume should have had it in his power to bring it. But that he against whom it was brought should have esteemed it as an honour, and should have recorded it in his diary as such, was worst of all.*

Even in this time of darkness, however, there were some who were "faithful found among the faithless;" and of these the first in time, and among the foremost in influence, was THOMAS BOSTON, author of "The Fourfold State," a work which was for

---

* "Autobiography of Dr. Alexander Carlyle," edited by J. H. Burton, p. 276.

nearly a century a household hand-book of theology among the Scottish peasantry. Born at Duns in 1676, he had, as a little boy, kept his father company when he was suffering in the jail of his native town for nonconformity. He was early brought under the power of the truth through the instrumentality of Henry Erskine, the father of the brothers Ebenezer and Ralph, who afterwards became the leaders of the Secession. He studied at the University of Edinburgh, and was licensed to preach in 1697, ordained over the little parish of Simprim in 1699, and transferred in 1707 to the parish of Ettrick, where he laboured till his death, in 1732. His sermons, of which a large number were published, had few of the graces of style, either in composition or delivery, though here and there in them we come upon epigrammatic and suggestive sentences. They were cast, withal, in the mould of the times, beginning with a painful opening up of the text and a statement of the doctrine to be insisted upon; then proceeding to an exposition of that through four or five heads, each having under it a series of particulars, and the whole followed by an application in which was a series of uses—as, for example, in one case, taken almost at random— use first, for information; use second, for trial; use third, for motive. They show also, in the prominence which they give to the covenant of works and the covenant of grace, the influence of that close intercourse between the Church of Scotland and the Church of Holland which was maintained before, during, and for some little time after the era of the Persecution. They are not, therefore, very attractive reading now, and will be resorted to only by those who are impelled to study them for some specific historic purpose. But they are full of Christ, and they are particularly noteworthy for the fulness and the freeness with which they press the offer of Christ and His salvation upon men.

While visiting one of his parishioners he came upon a book called "The Marrow of Modern Divinity," which had been written by one Edward Fisher, an Oxford scholar, and which had been brought, no one could tell how, when, or by whom, to the place immediately beneath the thatch in which it was discovered. There it had lain long, like the grain of wheat in the mummy's hand, but in the heart of Boston it took root and germinated. It was republished by one of Boston's friends, and twelve of the ministers of the Church were rebuked by the Assembly for giving their sanction to what Principal Hadow of St. Andrews alleged to be its

errors. In the words of the elder McCrie, "The Marrow doctrine, while it holds forth a complete salvation, presents a revealed ground—call it an offer, or promise, or deed of gift, or grant from God, warranting sinners *as such*, irrespective of any decree, or any qualification connected with the decree, to believe in, receive, and rest upon Christ for all they need for their recovery and happiness." *
Its author sometimes indulged in language which, unless qualified by what he had elsewhere said, might have been taken as implying that assurance is of the essence of faith, and that believers are not under obligation to obey the law. But from all such ambiguities and errors the Scottish "Marrow men," as they were called, kept themselves free, and the controversy which resulted from their publication of the book only issued in giving a wider publicity to the truth which Boston and his brethren proclaimed. "Christ," said he, "is given to mankind sinners indefinitely; not to the elect alone, but to sinners indefinitely elect or non-elect—sinners of the race of Adam, without exception." † Along with this he insisted most strenuously on the necessity of

---

* "The Evangelical Succession," Second Series, p. 95.
† *Ibid.*, 94.

the agency of the Holy Spirit, and on the absolute essentialness of holy living as the fruit and evidence of regeneration; and the result was seen in the quickening and sanctifying of many souls, not only in the parishes of the Marrow men, but all over the country.

And the wine of this new life burst the old wine-skin within which it was confined. For the Marrow controversy had really as much to do with the first Secession from the Scottish Church as Patronage, and the doctrines which I have just described were from the beginning the leading characteristics of the theological teachings of the Seceders. By the brothers EBENEZER and RALPH ERSKINE, especially, they were proclaimed with such power that they not only leavened the new denomination of which they were the leaders, but also did much to keep the lamp of truth from going out in many quarters of the land. The Secession itself dates from 1733; but Ebenezer Erskine had been in the ministry first at Portmoak, on the shore of Loch Leven, and afterwards at Stirling from 1703; and Ralph had been ordained in Dunfermline in 1711. They were, as I have already stated incidentally, the sons of Henry Erskine, who had been a sufferer both in

MODERATES AND EVANGELICALS.

England and Scotland from the tyranny of the Stuarts. They were educated at the University of Edinburgh, and were in every respect the peers of the ablest of their contemporaries. I have said enough about their secession in my introductory lecture, and must here confine myself to their influence as preachers. Of Ebenezer's discourses I have three volumes, and of Ralph's works ten, and all that I have said regarding Boston's sermons is equally true of these. Of the two, Ebenezer is the more stately, dignified, and measured, and Ralph the more fervid and full of unction, especially in the closing appeals, which excel everything of the kind which I have read of that age, except it may be those of Baxter; not certainly in literary style, but in the wonderful freeness and power with which he presses sinners to accept of Christ. One said of Ebenezer: "If you have never heard him preach, then you have never heard the Gospel in its majesty;" and after reading these applications at the end of Ralph's discourses I am almost disposed to say that if you have never read them, you have never read the Gospel in its freeness.

The sermons of both were fully written out, and were delivered *memoriter*; for Ebenezer says in the preface to one of them which he published, because he had been accused of saying something in it which he had not said, "It is my practice to write all that I have a mind to say in public. It is true, indeed, I do not pretend to such an exact memory as that I can confine myself in the delivery of everything in my notes without varying a word, but yet I used to be pretty exact that way." Of Ralph, one of his biographers says that, "for the most part, he wrote all and kept close to his notes" (that is, delivered *memoriter* precisely as he had written), "though if anything was given him in the moment of utterance he could avail himself of that also." He had a metaphysical mind, and excelled in making accurate distinctions—a quality which especially comes out in his work entitled "Faith no Fancy"—which even such philosophers as Hamilton and McCosh have spoken of with approbation. Singularly enough, in combination with that philosophic acumen, he had something also of the poetic faculty, and his Gospel Sonnets, despite the uncouthness of the rhymes and the oddness of the conceits which are constantly recurring, do yet contain some ingenious and striking thoughts, rising up, as in his verses on the "Contest in Heaven," to at least the verge of the sublime. They used to be very popular in rural Scotish homes, and in my boyhood I have heard them quoted with

MODERATES AND EVANGELICALS. 157

much unction by ministers in their addresses at the communion-table.

But for the Secession the influence of these two brothers would have been confined mainly to their own immediate neighbourhoods; but the travels and preachings incidental to the planting and organizing of new congregations in the new denomination took them to districts in all quarters of the land, and wherever they went their word was with power. Thus the very efforts of the Moderates to stamp out the flame only scattered the sparks in different directions, where the hearts of the people being already prepared for their reception, caught fire from them and burned with a devout enthusiasm.

While the Erskines and their coadjutors were labouring thus outside of the National Church, there were some eminent men of devoted Christian spirit and earnest Evangelical faith who deserve to be held in honourable remembrance for their noble work within its pale. Among these, perhaps the foremost place must be given to JOHN MACLAURIN, who was born in Argyleshire in 1693, educated in Glasgow and Leyden, and ordained at Luss, on the banks of Loch Lomond, in 1719, whence he was transferred to the North-west parish

in Glasgow, where he laboured till his death, in
1754. Some of his sermons were given to the
world by his son-in-law after his death, and they
must be classed among the greatest which were
published in the eighteenth century in the English
language. They are thoroughly Evangelical in their
substance, but much more attractive in their style
than those of Boston and the Erskines. They have
a grandeur and massiveness about them which are
quite remarkable, and they abound in original, profound, and suggestive thought. Dr. John Brown,
of Edinburgh, was fond of quoting from them, and
he usually introduced his citation by styling Maclaurin
" the first of our Scottish theologians," or " the profound Maclaurin ; " and of his discourse on " Glorying in the Cross," which Dr. Eadie has called " one
of the noblest in the language," Dr. Brown has said
that it exhibits " the glories of the cross of Christ
with a depth of spiritual understanding and feeling, and a force of argument and eloquence, seldom
equalled, and still more seldom combined." It is
free from all the mannerisms that were so common
in the preaching of that age, and marches on with
a stately step and solemn cadence worthy of its
theme. Ornate in language without being diffuse,
it is literally packed with meaning and lustrous with

clearness. We have no description of his manner, and cannot tell whether he read his discourses or delivered them from memory, but if given with anything like the condensed power with which it is written, such a passage as the following must have produced a great effect upon his hearers : " Here shine spotless justice, incomprehensible wisdom, and infinite love, all at once. None of these darkens or eclipses the others; every one of them gives a lustre to the rest. They mingle their beams with united eternal splendour—the just Judge, the merciful Father, and the wise Governor. No other object gives such a display of all these perfections; yea, all the objects we know give not such a display of any one of them. Nowhere does justice appear so awful, mercy so amiable, or wisdom so profound." See how every word tells. There is not a superfluous syllable. No epithets are used for padding. Every clause is a distinct thought. Thus the discourse moves on, gathering force as it goes, and well sustaining the weight even of such a theme. Indeed, if Maclaurin errs at all, it is in the condensation of his thought into the briefest expression. We do not feel that he is obscure as we *read*, but some of his listeners complained that he was difficult to follow as they *heard;* and we must not forget

Whately's caution, that "bulk is needful to digestion," and that judicious expansion is sometimes as powerful as a condensed epigram.

Maclaurin wrote also some valuable essays on such subjects as "The Prejudices of men against the Gospel" and "The Scripture Doctrine of Divine Grace;" and perhaps most interesting of all to us here is the fact that he was a correspondent of Jonathan Edwards, and was, like him, distinguished for the part he took in the revival of religion. When the fathers of the Secession so strangely quarrelled with Whitefield, because, during his visit to Scotland, he would not confine his ministrations to their pulpits, Maclaurin was full of joy at his work, and personally co-operated with those who carried on the movement which he began at Cambuslang. He was the chief contriver and promoter of the "concert for prayer" which had been acceded to by numbers both in Great Britain and America, and for which Edwards wrote one of his Treatises.*
There can be no doubt, therefore, that the influence of Maclaurin was very largely effective in keeping

---

* The title of Edwards's treatise is, "An humble Attempt to promote explicit Agreement and visible Union of God's People in Extraordinary Prayer for the Revival of Religion and the Advancement of Christ's Kingdom on Earth."

MODERATES AND EVANGELICALS.

the truth before the minds of the people in the west of Scotland during the early portion of the Moderate ascendancy. His writings have been recently republished under the editorship of the Rev. Dr. Goold, of Edinburgh, and they may still be studied with advantage by those who are preparing for or actually engaged in the work of the ministry.

Another of the earnest spirits in the Scottish Church at this time was JOHN WITHERSPOON, a lineal descendant of John Knox. He was born in 1722, educated at the University of Edinburgh, and settled first at Beith, in Ayrshire, then at Paisley, in Renfrewshire. He was an effective and popular preacher. His works on Justification and Regeneration are not unknown even in these days, and show the manner of man he was in the pulpit. But there was a vein of satire in him which came out in his volume entitled "Ecclesiastical Characteristics," in which the Moderates were held up to ridicule in the raciest style. But the sting of the wit was mostly in its truth, and that made him many enemies, who were in no degree mollified by a second volume, which he issued in defence of the first. On one occasion, however, his zeal outran his discretion, for hearing that on the night previous to the communion a set of youths held a meeting in

Paisley, at which they travestied the preaching and praying and the dispensation of the Supper, he delivered and published a sermon on the matter, giving the names of the offenders. This subjected him to an action at law, in which he was cast in costs; and shortly afterwards, having received an invitation to succeed Edwards in the presidency of Princeton College, he transferred himself to this country, where he did admirable service both in Church and State, and where his name is still held in honour as that of one of the signers of the Declaration of Independence. In him, as in JOHN MASON, the pulpits of Scotland and America touched each other. As in the vine of Joseph the branches ran over the wall, so the Scottish pulpit, through these noble men, spread over into this land and enriched it with its fruit.

Mention ought also to be made of such men as WILLISON of Dundee, the elder Sir HENRY MONCRIEFF, and others, but we must pass over them to make room for Dr. JOHN ERSKINE, of Edinburgh—not to be confounded with the Secession brothers of the same surname. Born in 1721, he was the son of a distinguished Scottish lawyer,* and was

---

* He was the author of the "Institutes of the Law of Scotland," and is still frequently called "The Scottish Blackstone."

MODERATES AND EVANGELICALS. 163

educated at the University of Edinburgh. He became minister of the parish of Kirkintilloch in 1744, and was transferred in 1758 to Edinburgh, where he was pastor first of New Greyfriars and finally of Old Greyfriars, in the latter of which he was the colleague of Principal Robertson, the historian. He was for long the leader of the Evangelicals in the Assembly, as Robertson was of the Moderates, and was distinguished alike for his ability as a preacher, his earnestness as a Christian, and his zeal for liberty as a citizen. He, too, was a correspondent of Edwards, and his was the first voice raised in Scotland against the monstrous injustice of the war which the government of Great Britain entered upon with her North American colonies, and which resulted in the independence of these United States. Hugh Miller says that his tract, "Shall I go to war with my American brethren?" is among the most powerful of his productions.[*] He published many able works in practical and doctrinal theology, and died in 1803. The father of Sir Walter Scott was one of his elders, and the most accurate and striking description of his public ministrations is given by the great novelist, very

---

[*] See the volume of Miller's works entitled "Headship of Christ," p. 147.

evidently from personal familiarity with that which he portrays, in the following paragraph, which I extract from "Guy Mannering:"* "The colleague of Dr. Robertson ascended the pulpit. His external appearance was not prepossessing. A remarkably fair complexion, strangely contrasted with a black wig without a grain of powder; a narrow chest, and a stooping posture; hands which, placed like props on either side of the pulpit, seemed necessary rather to support the person than to assist the gesticulation of the preacher—no gown, not even that of Geneva, a tumbled band, and a gesture which seemed scarce voluntary, were the first circumstances which struck a stranger. . . . A lecture was delivered, fraught with new, striking, and entertaining views of Scripture history—a sermon in which the Calvinism of the Kirk of Scotland was ably supported, yet made the basis of a sound system of practical morals which should neither shelter the sinner under the cloak of speculative faith or of peculiarity of opinion, nor leave him loose to the waves of unbelief and schism. Something there was of an antiquated turn of argument and metaphor but it only served to give zest and peculiarity

---

* "Guy Mannering," chap. xxxvii.

MODERATES AND EVANGELICALS. 165

to the style of elocution. The sermon was not read—a scrap of paper containing the heads of the discourse was occasionally referred to, and the enunciation, which at first seemed imperfect and embarrassed, became, as the preacher warmed in his progress, animated and distinct; and although the discourse could not be quoted as a correct specimen of pulpit eloquence, yet Mannering had seldom heard so much learning, metaphysical acuteness, and energy of argument brought into the service of Christianity. 'Such,' he said, going out of the church, 'must have been the preachers to whose unfearing minds and acute though sometimes rudely exercised talents we owe the Reformation.'"

The era of Moderate ascendancy was now approaching its zenith. It culminated in the famous debate on Missions in the General Assembly of 1796, of which Hugh Miller has given a graphic description in a series of valuable articles,[*] and which ended in the defeat of the friends of missions, who were led by Dr. Erskine, of whom we have just spoken. But a reaction was at hand, and the foremost place in the production of that must be given

---

[*] See "The Headship of Christ," *ubi supra*.

to Andrew Thomson, whose name is still venerated in his native land. He was born at Sanquhar in 1779, where his father was then minister of the parish church; and after some years spent at Markinch, in Fife, to which his father had removed, he was educated at the University of Edinburgh, and ordained to the ministry in 1802 at Sprouston, whence in 1808 he was removed to Perth, and thence in 1810 to Edinburgh, where he laboured first in the New Greyfriars Church, and afterwards in St. George's, until his death on his own doorstep in 1831, at the comparatively early age of fifty-two.

We have seen that the early Moderates devoted their attention to the cultivation of the graces of literature to the exclusion of the Gospel, and that the early Evangelicals, with but few conspicuous exceptions, confined themselves almost exclusively to the presentation of the Gospel, after a certain stereotyped and systematic fashion, with little or no regard to elegance of style or manner. Their discourses were bald in illustration, and broken up into fragments by numerous divisions and subdivisions, which prevented their attaining anything like climatic force. They were, besides, frequently delivered in a drawling, sing-song chant—a kind of "holy tone," as some irreverently called it—which was exceeding unnatural. Thus both parties had run into an extreme; and though, of the two, that of the Moderates was by far the worse, yet it has to be noted that the habits into which the Evangelicals had allowed themselves to fall tended to alienate the cultivated and refined from their ministrations.

However unnecessary it may seem to some in these days, there was then undeniable occasion for the protest against divorcing Evangelical truth from literary culture, which was so forcibly uttered by John Foster in his " Essay on the Aversion of Men of Taste to Evangelical Religion," and it must be confessed that in Scotland the Evangelicals had grievously erred in this particular. Even Ralph Erskine, whose general scholarship might have enabled him to excel in this department, instead of attempting to conciliate or attract cultivated minds by his attention to literary elegance, accounted it as an evidence of spiritual defection in the community that, as he said, "a world of people that come under the name of wits, and people of fine taste, are pleased with no sermons but such as are artificially decked with the flowers of gaudy rhetoric and tricky oratory, and this comes to be preferred to plain, powerful, spiritual preaching." * The good man refers to

---

* " Works," vol. ii. p. 250.

Paul's allegation to the Corinthians, that he had not come to them with "wisdom of words;" but in the same Epistle the same apostle declares that "he was made all things to all men, that he might by all means save some," and he would have been vastly wiser if, without in any way concealing the truth from view, he had striven by the "craft" of literary grace to catch such men with "guile."

Now it was the merit of Andrew Thomson that he brought back culture into the pulpit without in the least degree obscuring the Cross. The Gospel was always in the central and highest place in his discourses, but he clothed it in attractive forms, and was as eminent for the beauty of his composition as any of the best writers of his day; while the force of his eloquence was not surpassed save by the irresistible oratory of Chalmers. In point of fact, he began the work which Chalmers carried forward to its consummation, and there are few nobler names in the Ecclesiastical History of Scotland than those of these two men who were for a time contemporaries and friends. Neither of them would have placed literature above the Gospel, but both believed that they should serve the Lord with their best, and that it was their duty to set forth the doctrines of the Cross in the form best fitted to secure the attention

of their hearers. It had come to be the belief of a
large part of the community that to be an Evangelical was a mark of intellectual weakness and literary uncouthness; but in Thomson they beheld one
who in both of these respects was equal, if not superior, to the ablest lawyer or author in the land, and
they were in a manner compelled to respect the
position which he took.

While, therefore, the history of the Moderate
pulpit gives emphatic warning of the evil which
must ensue from the cultivation of the means as if
they were the end, that of the Evangelical pulpit
thus far is no less emphatic in its exposure of the
danger of neglecting altogether the proper adjustment of means to the end. There is here a case
for the application of the Saviour's words: "This
ought ye to have done, and not to have left the
other undone." The primary obligation is to preach
the Gospel—that ought to be done; the secondary
is not to neglect all proper means for so preaching
it that people will be drawn to listen to and believe
it—that ought not to be left undone. There will
be always offence in the Cross to the natural heart,
but the preacher's aim ought ever to be to secure
that he does not add to that by any negligence or
slovenliness or ungracefulness of his own either in

writing or in utterance. Reverting to the illustration which we have already used, "*the body is more than raiment*," but the raiment is not, therefore, of no consequence. With the Moderates too often there was nothing but raiment, and the result was a "tailor's dummy"—the garments exquisitely cut and admirably made, but no living form within them. With the Evangelicals far too frequently the raiment was ragged and torn, evoking the ridicule of the specutators, and leaving the living body bare in many places to the sarcasm of the scorner. Between these two extremes the ideal preacher will choose to adopt that dress for his message which shall best commend it to all classes, and defend it from all assault.

This was the course Dr. Andrew Thomson adopted, and for success in it he was singularly well endowed. He had a fine, manly presence, a wonderful ear for music, in which he was a great proficient, a voice of surpassing power and flexibility, and an exquisite sense of rhythmic harmony in the selection of words. He had a commanding intellect, a thorough knowledge of the world, unwavering faith in the great principles of the Gospel, and unflinching boldness combined with wonderful tact in the advocacy of unpopular truth. As Lord

Moncrieff said lately, "he was one of those orators who made your heart palpitate to hear."* Up till the time of his entering on the ministry of St. George's he had not been in the habit of writing his discourses, but, after premeditation, had trusted to his natural fluency, when heated by the fire of the pulpit, to supply him with the expressions which he needed. But when he went to his new charge, and sought to gather round him the best minds in the city, he changed his method and wrote two discourses every week, which he read from his manuscript in the pulpit. But the freedom of his off-hand manner remained, so that even when reading his eye was everywhere among the people, and he kept himself thoroughly *en rapport* with them. It was of immense consequence just then, not only that he should give diligent preparation to his discourses, but also that *it should be seen and known of all that he had done so*, and the result showed that he had judged wisely, for the effect of his attention to these matters was very soon apparent. Lockhart, in his "Peter's Letters to his Kinsfolk," has described it thus: "I am assured that church-going was a thing comparatively out

---

* Address at the Centenary of Chalmers in 1880.

of fashion among the fine folks of the New Town
of Edinburgh till this man was removed from a
church he formerly held in the Old Town, and
established under the splendid dome of St. George's.
Only two or three years have elapsed since this
change took place, and yet, though he was at first
received with no inconsiderable coolness by the self-
complacent gentry of the new parish, and although
he adopted nothing that ordinary people would have
supposed likely to overcome this coolness, he has
already entirely subdued their prejudices, and
enjoys at this moment a degree of favour among all
classes of his auditors such as very seldom falls to
the share of such a man in such a place."* And
having seen the great efficacy of this alteration of
his method of preparing for the pulpit and preaching in it, he would not allow himself to be tempted
back by any considerations of personal ease to his
former practice. Perhaps he had begun to discover, even before his removal to St. George's, that
there may be a fluency which is ultimately fatal to
pulpit power. In any case, he prepared to the last
with utmost care; and a good story is told of him
in this connection which I repeat here because it

---

* " Peter's Letters to his Kinsfolk," vol. iii. pp. 79, 80.

MODERATES AND EVANGELICALS. 173

may fix in your memories this great lesson of his example. A minister who was a keen angler once said to him, " I wonder you spend so much time on your sermons, with your ability and ready speech. Many's the time I've both written a sermon and killed a salmon before breakfast." " Well, sir," replied Thomson, " I would rather have eaten your salmon than listened to your sermon ! "*

He believed in the utilization of the press as well as of the pulpit, and through the pages of *The Christian Instructor*—a monthly magazine of which he was the founder and first editor, and in which he was greatly assisted by his Dissenting friend, Dr. Thomas McCrie, the biographer of Knox —he did much to mould the religious opinion of his time, and to secure the ultimate triumph of the Evangelical party in the Scottish Church. But it was on the platform that his most splendid oratorical victories were won. For that kind of eloquence he had many qualifications. He had a clear perception of the weak points in an adversary's case and the strong positions in his own. He had great fluency of speech and thorough command of himself. He had the richest humour, and a stock of anecdotes of

---

* "Life of Andrew Thomson, DD.," p. 24. Jean L. Watson.

the raciest sort, which seemed to come up just where they could be most effectively employed, reminding us in this of Guthrie more than any other of his successors. He had a keen vein of satire, too, which could be playful and harmless on occasion as summer lighting, but which was often also forked and deadly, like the bolt that rends the forest oak. Frequently in the Assembly and on the platform he spoke for two or three hours at a stretch; and when some one remarked on the length of time he had in one such instance kept up the attention of the people, he replied, "Whenever I see them get dull I throw in a story. I consider a story has an effect for twenty minutes."[*] Sometimes he gave way to irritability and vehemence, for he had the sensitive organization of the orator; but he was always ready to make reparation or retraction if he had been unjust, for he had the spirit of the Christian. He took a prominent part in the once famous Apocrypha controversy, occasioned by the circulation in certain places by the British and Foreign Bible Society of the Apocrypha bound up with the Word of God, and he was the fearless advocate of the emancipation of the slave. Indeed,

---

[*] "Life of Andrew Thomson, D.D.," *ubi supra*, p. 82.

one speech made by him on that subject became historic, and long as this lecture has been, I must detain you a very few minutes more while I give you some idea of its power.

It was in October 1830. A great public meeting had been convened in Edinburgh, with a view to the securing of the gradual abolition of slavery in the British Colonies, and Francis Jeffrey had made a speech in which he moved that a petition be sent to Parliament praying that every child of slaves born after the 31st of December 1831 should be declared free. Thomson was present, but to the surprise of every one he had taken his seat in the body of the house and not on the platform. When the motion was put he rose, and was immediately requested by the Lord Provost, who was in the chair, to go upon the platform; but, with a look of drollery on his face, he said, "I cannot do that, for I am going to speak against your resolutions." The audience could not understand *his* opposing the abolition of slavery; but when he went on to explain that he was opposed to gradual emancipation, and insisted on its being immediate, enforcing that view with a power and pathos quite beyond his usual eloquence, he fairly captured the meeting. He was importuned to make a motion for immediate emancipation, but the confusion became so great that the Lord Provost left the chair, and after a while it was agreed to adjourn to another day, when both parties should have it out. When the appointed time arrived he had to confront a divided house. There were some who were sincerely opposed to his proposal, and there were others, principally young men from the University, who were simply bent on mischief. But one who was present says: "In less than twenty minutes the entire meeting was with him, including the youthful malcontents, whom I was amused and delighted to observe laughing as heartily at his bright and genial humour, and cheering as enthusiastically his reiterated bursts of eloquence, as any in the hall."[*] He continued for a long while, and he concluded with the following passage—a speech which was so irresistible in its force that not only Edinburgh but the whole country was moved, and the cry for immediate emancipation, which he was the first to raise, was echoed and re-echoed until it entered the British House of Commons, and that Act was passed which will stand in history for ever, side by

---

[*] "Life of Andrew Thomson, D.D.," *ubi supra*, pp. 113, 114.

side with the Emancipation Proclamation of Abraham Lincoln, as the beginning of justice to the coloured race.

Here is the peroration : " As a proof of the necessity of gradual emancipation, Mr. C—— tells us the old story of a man who had been confined for thirty years in the Bastille, and who, when liberated at the destruction of that horrid State prison, became more miserable by the suddenness of his transition, and adds that his liberators would have been more rational and more humane had they provided an asylum to receive him. This I agree with Mr. C—— in thinking they ought to have done; but the analogy does not hold, for instead of proposing that the slaves should be turned adrift and cared for no more, we propose that such arrangements shall be made as are suited to the exigencies of their condition. This is what our petition prays for along with their emancipation. It is what they are entitled to in equity as well as in compassion, and far be it from us to say or do anything that would disparage such a claim. But really Mr. C—— does not seem to entertain adequate ideas on the subject. ' His eye,' says he, ' could not bear the effulgence of day, because its physical structure had accommodated itself to the glimmering of a gloomy cell.' It is really trifling with the subject to talk thus gravely on the man's eye being unable to bear the daylight, for that is the plain meaning of the words. Why, sir, a green shade would have answered the purpose; and then, sir, I would infinitely rather be a free man with my eyes hermetically sealed against all the beauties of the earth, and all the magnificence of the firmament, than I would be a slave with my eyes wide open to look upon my chains that were never to be broken, and upon my taskmasters who were never to have done with oppressing me, and upon my dearest kindred who were either enjoying a blessing from which I was for ever excluded, or to be my fellow-sufferers without hope, under the basest and bitterest of all human degradation.

"But if you push me, and still urge the argument of insurrection and bloodshed, for which you are far more indebted to fancy than to fact, as I have shown you, then I say, be it so. I repeat that maxim, taken from a heathen book, but pervading the whole Book of God, 'Fiat justitia ruat cœlum.' Righteousness, sir, is the pillar of the universe. Break down that pillar and the universe falls into ruin and desolation; but preserve it, and though the fair fabric be dilapidated—it may be rebuilt and repaired—it will be rebuilt and repaired, and restored to all its pristine strength and magnificence and beauty. If there must be violence, let it even come, for it will soon pass away; let it come and rage its little hour, since it is to be succeeded by lasting freedom and prosperity and happiness. Give me the hurricane rather than the pestilence. Give me the hurricane, with its thunder, and its lightning, and its tempest; give me the hurricane, with its partial and temporary devastations, awful though they be; give me the hurricane, with its purifying, healthful, salutary effects; give me that hurricane infinitely rather than the noisome pestilence whose path is never crossed, whose silence is never disturbed, whose progress is never arrested by one sweeping blast from the heavens; which walks peacefully and sullenly through the length and breadth of the land, breathing poison into every heart and carrying havoc into every home; enervating all that is strong, defacing all that is beautiful, and casting its blight over the fairest and happiest scenes of human life; and which, from day to day, and from year to year, with intolerant and interminable malignity, sends its thousands and its tens of thousands of hapless victims into the ever-yawning and never-satisfied grave." *

---

* " Life of Andrew Thomson, D.D.," *ubi supra*, pp. 85–88.

After hearing one read such an outburst of eloquence we are reminded of the saying of Æschines: "If such be its effect when repeated by another, what must it have been to have heard it from his own burning lips?"

NOTE.

NOTE. See page 146.
The Literary Eminence of the Moderates.

The highest estimate of the literary service rendered by the Moderate party to Scotland that I have seen is that of Dr. Peter Bayne, in his "Life and Letters of Hugh Miller," which I here append, that I may not seem to be guilty of doing them an injustice. I cannot agree with all that Dr. B. has said in their behalf, and as I rewrite his sentences I try to imagine what Hugh Miller himself would have exclaimed had he dreamed that such a panegyric on *them* should have found a place in a memoir of *him*; but let it be allowed "*quantum valeat.*"

"One knows not where to look in ecclesiastical history for a party of which the nucleus consisted of clergymen so loyal to the higher aims of the human spirit, so ardent in its love of knowledge, so free from sectarian bigotry, so genial and tolerant in its habits of thought and feeling, as the Scottish Moderates. Under their influence the rugged face of old Scottish Presbyterianism mantled with a smile of calm and bright intelligence, which drew upon Scotland the astonished gaze of Europe. Robertson was in his own day known in Paris almost as well as in Edinburgh; his books had an honoured place in the library of Voltaire, and there is no university in Europe at this hour in which his name is not held in high esteem. He was the friend and historical rival of Hume, who, *except* in his speculative philosophy, was a true Moderate. If it is to be held a disgrace to the party that its chiefs were in friendly intercourse with the prince of iconoclasts, we ought to remember that there went out also from the Moderate camp those champions who, both in the field of pure philosophy and in that of apologetic divinity challenged Hume to the combat, and in the judgment of a world certainly not prejudiced in favour of parsons and against philosophers, put Hume to his mettle. I allude, of course, to Principal Campbell and Dr. Reid. The philosophy of Reid assaulted Hume along his whole line of battle. Interpreted as Hamilton interprets it, that philosophy is one in fundamentals with every great constructive system of spiritual thought from that of Plato to that of Kant. It consists, in one word, of an intelligent and critical appeal to the common spiritual nature—call it *communis sensus*, call it reason, call it intuition, call it what you will—of the human race. This remains, and must remain, whatever the dialect in which you express it, the sole philosophical refuge from universal scepticism. It is characteristic of the noble tolerance and candour and high intellectual serenity of those old Moderates, that Reid forwarded to Hume in manuscript his reply to the philosopher. A finer proof of a desire to deal fairly with an opponent, and of an absolute rejection of every weapon of personal or vituperative controversy, cannot be imagined. But the Moderate party of the Scottish Church can claim not only Campbell, Reid, and Robertson, but one who would now be placed by many higher than either of the three—the author of 'The Wealth of Nations.' Smith's 'Theory of Moral Sentiments' is a thoroughly Moderate book; moderate in its eloquent and high-toned moralizing, moderate in its lucidity and logical coherence, and also, perhaps, in its want of intensity, enthusiasm, and penetrating, exhaustive power. It was under the genial auspices of the Moderate party that the Scottish universities attained to such renown that young Palmerston and Russell went from England to study in their halls. It was under the auspices of the Moderate party that Edinburgh became the Weimar of Great Britain, that the most important publications of the time in Europe—the *Edinburgh Review*

and *Blackwood* and the *Quarterly*—arose. When John Murray conceived the scheme of the *Quarterly*, his first step was to start for the north to confer with Scott and the literati of Edinburgh. The leaders of Moderatism showed a wise and nobly patriotic spirit in never trying to exclude Seceders from the universities. They indulged the shrewd preference of the Scottish commonalty for 'college-bred ministers,' and spared their country the stunted and acrid growths of illiterate Dissent. It may doubtless be argued that Moderatism was itself but part of a wider phenomenon, to wit, the prevalence and predominance throughout society, not Scottish and English alone, but European, during the eighteenth century, of literary and scientific tastes and ambitions as contrasted with those of a religious nature; but the truth of this statement does not neutralize the fact that, under the reign of Moderatism, a literary and philosophical lustre was thrown over Scotland, for which, in the mere epoch of dominant Evangelicanism, we look in vain."
—*Life and Letters of Hugh Miller*, vol. ii. pp. 187-189.

There is much in these sentences to provoke criticism and challenge dissent. They give an exaggerated impression, not so much by putting in that which did not exist as by leaving out a great deal which subtracted from the undeniable excellences of the party in many respects. One needs not go further than the volume of Miller's own articles on "The Headship of Christ" in proof of what we have said; but the quotations already given in these pages from McCosh, Lindsay, and Alexander, put some deep shadows into the picture which Dr. Bayne has drawn. In literature and philosophy the Moderates were worthy of all the praise they here receive, but they were a *religious* party, and must be finally judged by their influence on the religious life of the land.

VI.

THOMAS CHALMERS.

AT the time of Dr. Andrew Thomson's death, THOMAS CHALMERS, the greatest of Scottish preachers, had been for some years Professor of Theology in the University of Edinburgh, and had, indeed, finished that unique and most instructive succession of pastorates which comprised what may be termed the ministerial portion of his wonderful career. He was born in Anstruther, in the county of Fife, on the 17th of March 1780, and after an ordinary course of instruction at the parish school he entered the University of St. Andrews at the age of twelve. His juvenility made it impossible for him to take the full advantage of the classical portion of the curriculum, which then extended over the first two years of the college course, and it was not until the third year of his undergraduate life that his intellect really awoke. The first study which thoroughly interested him was mathematics, in which he became highly proficient, and for which he retained a liking till the last. But he was drawn almost as eagerly to the departments of ethics and politics, for it was the seething time of the French Revolution, and he was well-nigh swept from his moorings, such as they were at that time, by Godwin's work on Political Justice.

From such a fate, however, he was saved by the influence on him, in the first year of his theological course, of Jonathan Edwards's famous " Treatise on the Freedom of the Will," which gave him such views of the personality, the greatness, the love, the wisdom, and the all-pervading energy of God, that he described himself long after as having " spent a twelvemonth in a sort of mental elysium," and said " that not a single hour elapsed in which the overpoweringly impressive imagination did not stand out bright before the inward eye; and that his custom was to wander early in the morning into the country, that amid the quiet scenes of nature he might luxuriate in the glorious conception." It was at that time the custom in the University of St. Andrews that all the members assembled daily in the public hall for morning and evening prayers, which were conducted by the theological students in regular order; and such was the eloquence with which on these occasions Chalmers was accustomed to express his sense of the glory of the Divine attributes, that the citizens of the place flocked into the assembly-room when they knew that it was his turn to pray. But though there was in these effusions a great coruscation of eloquent dissertation, there was no sense of spiritual need. They were sincere so far as they went; but they were the intellectual efforts of a Deist, and they had nothing in them of the humble supplications of a sinner, or of the lofty communion of a saint.

After passing through his theological curriculum he was licensed to preach the Gospel on the 31st of July 1799, while he was yet but nineteen years of age. The law of the Church at that time required that a licentiate should be twenty-one years old, but it was set aside in his case on the ground that " he was a lad of pregnant parts;" and he virtually observed the law, after all, for though thus early approved by his Presbytery, he does not seem to have been in any haste to preach. He spent two sessions, after license, at the University of Edinburgh in the study of mathematics and chemistry, and it was not until the 2nd of November 1802 that he was advanced to the pastorate of the parish of Kilmany. Before that date he had been for a few months assistant to the minister of Cavers, but he did not reside in the parish, and satisfied his conscience with a weekly visit for the purpose of preaching the sermon that was required of him. Nor were things much better after his ordination. His ambition at that time was entirely academical. He had set his heart on becoming Professor of Mathematics in the University of St. Andrews, and during the first year of his ministry he officiated as assistant professor, doing all the work of the chair, and then repairing to Kilmany on the Saturday to go through the round of Sabbath duty, after which he returned to St. Andrews on the Monday morning. The second year the mathematical professor dispensed with his services—Chalmers thought from jealousy—and therefore he set up for himself as an extra-mural lecturer. But though he keenly felt what he believed to be a personal slight in the matter of the professorship, his conscience was no way sensitive, as yet, concerning the demands of the pastorate. He believed that after the satisfactory discharge of his parish duties he might have five days of the week uninterrupted for the prosecution of any scientific work to which his taste might incline him. In short, he looked upon his ministerial labours as lighter things, to which he might devote the leisure which he could command from more important pursuits.

But a wonderful revolution from all this was soon to be effected. A speech delivered by him in the General Assembly of 1809, on the subject of the augmentation of the stipends of the clergy, attracted general attention for its ability, its humour, its " canniness," and its indications of genius and power, so that Andrew Thomson asked him to write for the *Christian Instructor*, and Brewster requested him to contribute to the *Edinburgh Encyclopædia*. For the latter of these publications he undertook to write the article " Christianity," and the preparation of that dissertation, following close upon a series of severe bereavements and a long and serious illness, in the course of which he had become deeply impressed with the importance of spiritual concerns, led to a change in his religious sentiments which, after his perusal of Wilberforce's " Practical View of Christianity," resulted in his conversion to Christ.

From that moment his whole character and work were transfigured and glorified. He laid himself upon the altar, and the altar not only sanctified but energized and ennobled the gift. Formerly the Bible was scarcely ever in his hand, now it was the theme of his constant and delighted study. No longer now did he regard the work of the ministry as a sort of extra to which he might turn as a relaxation in the interludes of more important labours, but it became the one great, absorbing enterprise of his life. And whereas before he had restricted himself to the enforcement of the precepts of morality, and had assured his people " that all the deficiencies of their imperfect virtue would be supplied by the atonement and propitiation of Christ," he was now convinced that " in the system of 'Do this and live,' no peace, and even no true and worthy obedience, can ever be attained;" it is " Believe in the Lord Jesus Christ and thou shalt be saved."

The result was that now the great feature of his sermons was the earnestness with which he held forth Christ and His salvation as God's free gift, which it was the sinner's privilege and duty at once and most gratefully to accept. Nay, not satisfied with doing that in the body of his discourse, he would often, after the concluding devotional exercises, and before the benediction, break out anew into entreaty, as if unwilling to let any one go until he had laid hold of Jesus Christ as freely offered to him in the Gospel. Those who have recovered from a long illness know how new and fresh everything looked to them when they first went out to gaze upon the face of Nature. Now, after his conversion, something like that in the case of the Scriptures and that Gospel which is the main burden of their testimony, was experienced by Chalmers, and that fresh newness he caught and preserved in the sermons which he wrote at that time, and which were afterwards given, just as they were originally written, to rapt and awe-struck hearers in Glasgow and Edinburgh. He devoted himself wholly to this work, and very soon the profiting appeared unto all men. For not only did the church become crowded with hearers drawn from all the parishes around, but conversions were frequent, and that which he did not succeed in accomplishing by mere ethical teaching was wrought by the spirit of God through his uplifting of the cross of Christ before his hearers.

This was "a crucial instance." If any man could have succeeded in the improvement of his fellows by the simple enforcement of morality it was Chalmers; for he was great on all sides of his nature, and had, besides, that subtle, indescribable thing which we call genius, and which makes everything magnetic which it touches. But even in his case the effort was a failure; while, on the other hand, so soon as he began to proclaim the Gospel as Paul preached it, he found it to be " the power of

God unto salvation unto every one that believeth." Here is his own testimony in his parting address to the inhabitants of Kilmany, which I quote not only as a specimen of his well-known style, but because it has fallen a little out of sight in these last days, and we need to be anew reminded of the truth which it emphasizes. The passage is somewhat long, but its importance will justify me in giving it in full:—

"And here I cannot but record the effect of an actual though undesigned experiment which I prosecuted for upwards of twelve years among you. For the greater part of that time I could expatiate on the meanness of dishonesty, on the villany of falsehood, on the despicable arts of calumny; in a word, upon all those deformities of character which awaken the natural indignation of the human heart against the pests and the disturbers of human society. Now, could I, upon the strength of these warm expostulations, have got the thief to give up his stealing, and the evil speaker his censoriousness, and the liar his deviations from truth, I should have felt all the repose of one who had gotten his ultimate object. It never occurred to me that all this might have been done, and yet the soul of every hearer have remained in full alienation from God; and

that even could I have established in the bosom of
one who stole such a principle of abhorrence at the
meanness of dishonesty that he was prevailed upon
to steal no more, he might still have retained a
heart as completely unturned to God, and as totally
unpossessed by a principle of love to Him as before.
In a word, though I might have made him a more
upright and honourable man, I might have left him
as destitute of the essence of religious principle as
ever. *But the interesting fact is that during the
whole of that period, in which I made no attempt
against the natural enmity of the mind to God;*
while I was inattentive to the way in which this
enmity is dissolved, even by the free offer on the
one hand, and the believing acceptance on the other,
of the Gospel salvation; while Christ, through whose
blood the sinner who by nature stands afar off is
brought near to the heavenly Lawgiver whom he
has offended, was scarcely ever spoken of, or spoken
of in such a way as stripped Him of all the importance of His character and His offices, even at this
time I certainly did press the reformations of honour
and truth and integrity among my people, but *I
never once heard of any such reformations having
been effected among them. If there was anything at
all brought about in this way, it was more than ever*

I got any account of. I am not sensible that all the vehemence with which I urged the virtues and the proprieties of social life had the weight of a feather on the moral habits of my parishioners. And it was not till I got impressed by the utter alienation of the heart in all its desires and affections from God; it was not till reconciliation to Him became the distinct and the prominent object of my ministerial exertions; it was not till I took the Scriptural way of laying the method of reconciliation before them; it was not till the free offer of forgiveness through the blood of Christ was urged upon their acceptance, and the Holy Spirit given through the channel of Christ's mediatorship to all who ask Him was set before them, as the unceasing object of their dependence and their prayers; in one word, it was not till the contemplations of my people were turned to these great and essential elements in the business of a soul providing for its interests with God, and the concerns of its eternity, that I ever heard of any of those subordinate reformations which I aforetime made the earnest and the zealous, but I am afraid, at the same time, the ultimate object of my earlier ministrations. Ye servants whose scrupulous fidelity has now attracted the notice of, and drawn forth in my hearing a delightful testimony from your masters, what mischief you would have done had your zeal for doctrines and sacraments been accompanied by the sloth and the remissness, and what, in the prevailing tone of moral relaxation, is accounted the allowable purloining, of your earlier days! But a sense of your heavenly Master's eye has brought another influence to bear upon you, and while you are thus striving to adorn the doctrine of God your Saviour in all things, you may, poor as you are, reclaim the great ones of the land to the acknowledgment of the faith. You have at least taught me that to preach Christ is the only effective way of preaching morality in all its branches, and out of your humble cottages have I gathered a lesson which I pray God I may be enabled to carry with all its simplicity into a wider theatre, and to bring with all the power of its subduing efficacy upon the vices of a more crowded population."*

"What shall a man do that cometh after the king?" You can never repeat Chalmers's experiment under more favourable circumstances, and why should you try to go again through that part of

---

* "Memoir of the Life and Writings of Thomas Chalmers, DD.," vol. i. pp. 434-436. Rev. William Hanna, LL.D.

it which on his own showing was an absolute failure? Take his word for it. This is the conclusion of the whole matter, " To preach Christ is the only effective way of preaching morality in all its branches ; " and when you enter on your ministry, begin it on that principle. Leave all philosophizings, and speculations, and reasonings about science, falsely so called, and preach Christ. The theme is old, but the new man makes everything new ; and that old theme, enforced by a *new* man who has passed through an experience like that of Chalmers, will be as fresh as the most advanced thought of the age with which multitudes are so enamoured. A few years ago there was a considerable outcry for a revival of ethical teaching in the pulpit, because of the occurrence of repeated instances of defalcation and defection among those connected with Christian churches. But that was not what was needed. The doctors were all agreed that these violations of trust were a symptom of something; but as to what that something was they differed. In the light of this experience of Chalmers, however, those were right who affirmed that their dishonesties were an indication not of too little preaching of ethics, but of too little preaching of Christ, and I rejoiced in the brave and ringing words on that aspect of the case which came from the beloved and honoured brother who then sat in the homiletic chair of this seminary.* May I entreat you to bear this test case of Chalmers's continually in mind, and never to allow yourselves to be diverted by any influence whatever from the insistence upon those great central truths which revolve around the cross of the Lord Jesus Christ.

From Kilmany, Chalmers was called to Glasgow, where, on the 21st of July 1815, he was installed as pastor of the Tron Church, and whence, in August 1819, he was transferred, in the same city, to the new parish of St. John's, which was virtually created for him. In the former of these he did in his own way a work very similar to that which was accomplished at the same time by Thomson in Edinburgh. He brought back the cultured and refined into the allegiance of the Cross without alienating the common people. His discourses were, in their leading thoughts, intellectual and abstract, and so fitter for the educated than the uneducated; but the Christian experience with which they were pervaded, the vivid imagination by which they were occasionally illuminated, and the

---

* The Rev. Professor Hoppin, in *The New Englander*.

whirlwind of earnestness with which they were delivered, carried the most untutored in his audience with him as if by storm; and the stories which are told of their effects would seem almost incredible but for the character of the witnesses who agree in their attestation of them.

It was at this time that he delivered his famous Astronomical Discourses, which, whatever may be said either of the objection which he sought to meet, or of the argument by which he met it, must be pronounced unrivalled for the grandeur and amplitude of their sweep through the depths of space, and for what John Foster called "the brilliant glow of a blazing eloquence" with which they displayed the sublime poetry of the heavens. They were first preached on Thursday afternoons, and they drew merchants from their places of business at the most important hour of the day in such numbers that there was often no standing room to be obtained within the church. Dr. Wardlaw has given the following description of the scene: " Suppose the congregation assembled—pews filled with sitters, and aisles to a great extent with standers. They wait in eager expectation. The preacher appears. The devotional exercises of praise and prayer having been gone through with unaffected simplicity and

earnestness, the entire assembly set themselves for
the treat, with feelings very diverse in kind, but
all eager and intent. There is a hush of dead
silence. The text is announced, and he begins.
Every countenance is up, every eye bent with fixed
intentness on the speaker. As he kindles, the
interest grows. Every breath is held, every cough
is suppressed, every fidgety movement is settled ;
every one, riveted himself by the spell of the impassioned and entrancing eloquence, knows how
sensitively his neighbour will resent the very slightest
disturbance. Then, by-and-by, there is a pause.
The speaker stops to gather breath, to wipe his
forehead, to adjust his gown, and purposely too, and
wisely, to give the audience as well as himself a
moment or two of relaxation. The moment is
embraced ; there is a free breathing, suppressed
coughs get vent, postures are changed, there is a
universal stir, as of persons who could not have
endured the constraint much longer. The preacher
bends forward, his hand is raised, all is again
hushed. The same stillness and strain of un-
relaxed attention is repeated, more intent still, it
may be, than before, as the interest of the subject
and the speaker advance. And so for perhaps four
or five times in the course of a sermon there is the

relaxation and the 'at it again,' till the final winding up."*

To many, no doubt, he was in all this only like one "who had a pleasant voice, and could play well on an instrument," but Dr. Wardlaw adds that there was abundant proof " that in the highest sense his labour was not in vain in the Lord, and that the truths which with so much fearless fidelity and impassioned earnestness he delivered went in many instances farther than the ear or the intellect; that they reached the heart, and by the power of the Spirit of God turned it to God."

In St. John's Church he inaugurated and superintended what was perhaps the greatest and most effective parochial organization which the Christian Church has ever seen in operation. His idea was that the poor of the parish, that is, all the poor resident within its boundaries, should be supported, not by local rates, but by the voluntary contributions of the inhabitants as they entered the church; and though the population numbered more than ten thousand, and most of them were weavers, labourers, and factory workers, he yet succeeded for three

---

* "Memoir of the Life and Writings of Thomas Chalmers, D.D.," *ubi supra*, vol. ii. p 158.

years not only in supplying the wants of the poor, but also in erecting and supporting most excellent schools; and, indeed, after he had left the parish, and so long as the machinery which he originated remained in operation, the results were such as to astonish all beholders. His church was a perfect beehive, without any drones—the realization of John Wesley's ideal, "at work, all at work, and always at work;" and busiest of all was the pastor himself, so that an assistant was engaged to relieve him of some of his onerous duties.

This assistant was the famous EDWARD IRVING, whose name has once more come into prominence through the recent publication of the Carlyle Reminiscences, Letters, and Memoirs, and whose reputation is the only one, in my judgment, that comes unsullied out of the mess which these revelations have made. Indeed, there are few passages in modern literature more touching than that which describes him sitting by his friend on the lone Scottish moor, and coming to the sad discovery that his companion had drifted away from his faith in Christianity as a supernatural revelation. Willingly would I linger a little over that gifted son of genius, not unworthy in many respects to stand by the side of Chalmers, and whose juxtaposition to him here serves to bring out so marked a contrast, and to point so significant a warning. Chalmers, with all his soaring imagination, always walked in the practical, but Irving was visionary and romantic, to the entire neglect of the practical and practicable. His mental as well as his physical vision was oblique, and he was always apt to fly off at some tangent of truth, because he was not centripetally balanced. When he went to London to begin his work there he said, "There are a few things which bind me to the world, and but very few; one is to make a demonstration for a higher style of Christianity, something more magnanimous than this age affects, God knoweth with what success." And for a time, despite some eccentricities and mistakes, he was a great power in the metropolis on the side of truth and righteousness, gathering round him multitudes of men of highest culture and influence in that great city. But, by-and-by, he became connected with the Albany Conference, and devoted himself almost exclusively to prophetic studies, becoming editor of the *Morning Watch*, and taking a foremost place among those who gave themselves to the mapping out of "times and seasons." From that hour his influence began to wane. Then came the sad scenes of the Tongues, then the organization of the Catholic Apostolic

Church, and then his depth, as of one burned up with some inner volcanic fire. Thus an influence which might have been lasting for good went out in the origination of a new denomination which has attempted to combine the symbolism of the Old Testament with the doctrine of the New, but has had little or no effect upon the solution of the great questions or the guidance of the great movements of the age. The contrast between that denomination, which is the outcome of Irving's work, and the Free Church of Scotland, which is the outcome of the work of Chalmers, is suggestive of many things, but of none to you more useful than of the danger of losing sight of the duty of the present in the exclusive study of the future. Had Irving set himself with anything like the devotion of Chalmers to the " excavation " of the heathen in some district of London, instead of curiously prying into the unfulfilled prophecies of the future, there might have been no tongues, but there would have been more good effected, and the Church might not have had to mourn over the aberration of one of her noblest sons. It is the aggressiveness of the Church that is to keep it orthodox, and whenever schemes of prophetic fulfilment, or indeed speculations of any sort, take the place of efforts for the evangelization of the unconverted, we may look out for the uprising of some form of Irvingism.

But I must return to Chalmers. The continuous strain and excitement of his work at St. John's began to tell upon his strength, and that moved him, much to the regret of all the citizens of Glasgow, to accept the chair of Moral Philosophy in the University of St. Andrews, where he spent the years from 1823 till 1828, and whence, at the latter date, he was transferred to the Professorship of Theology in Edinburgh, an office which he held till the disruption of the Church in 1843.

This is not the place to enter upon a discussion of what came afterwards to be known as "The Ten Years' Conflict" between the courts of the Church and the civil courts of the land, which issued in the formation of the Free Church. Let it suffice for me to state that Chalmers had entered most heartily into the prosecution of an effort for church extension whereby two hundred new churches had been erected in destitute localities; and now out of the struggle which he and his coadjutors maintained there came a yet larger measure of church extension, though not precisely in the way that he first anticipated. The effort to secure the spiritual independence of the Church was, especially in its later stages, fully more a religious revival than a political conflict; and it was because he valued the spiritual as the end to the attainment of which the establishment was regarded by him as only a means, that he became so willing at length to sever the connection which bound him to the State. So late as the spring of 1838 he had delivered in London, amid great *éclat*, and with the countenance of bishops and statesmen, a course of lectures in defence of the establishment of the Church by the State, and many have accused him of inconsistency in seceding only five years later from the State Church himself; but there was in reality no change in his way of looking at the subject. At a later date he said, " Who cares about the Free Church compared with the Christian good of the people of Scotland ? Who cares about any Church but as an instrument of Christian good ? " * and these were his sentiments all through. He valued the establishment of a Church by the State only as a means of securing the spiritual welfare of the people ; and when he found that he was baffled in his efforts to get at the people for their good by an interference from the civil

---

* " Memoir of the Life and Writings of Thomas Chalmers, DD.," p. 168. Norman L. Walker.

courts, which was declared to be an inevitable consequence of the establishment of the Church by the State, then, with characteristic earnestness and decision, and with perfect consistency, he severed his connection with the State Church, that he might thereby the better accomplish the great spiritual end which he had in view. Personally I believe that the connection of a Church with the State is always and everywhere pernicious, and I have no sympathy with the arguments of Chalmers's famous lectures on the subject, but that does not prevent me from doing justice to his position, or from perceiving his thorough consistency with himself in the course which he adopted.

At the Disruption Chalmers became Professor of Theology to the Free Church, and to the end of his days he had around him a circle of loving and devoted students, all of whom were fired with enthusiasm which they had caught from his lips. Indeed that, next to his thorough grasp and clear exposition of the great doctrines of experimental theology, was his special forte as a teacher. He did not deal in learned disquisitions or subtle discussions. He was not so much an instructor as a quickener. The other professors laid the materials in the minds of the students, but he brought and struck the match which kindled these materials into a flame that burned with an energy kindred to his own. Each of them went forth not only with an ardent affection for his teacher in his heart, but also eager to follow him in his great work for the Christian welfare of the people of Scotland—nor of Scotland only, but of the world; for at St. Andrews Duff was fired with missionary zeal under his influence, and in Edinburgh some of the greatest of our modern ministers and missionaries were stirred into consecrated enthusiasm by his fervid utterances.

But his most interesting enterprise was yet to come. Still yearning to get " the common people " into the Church, he set about the "excavation," after his own territorial plan, of that district of Edinburgh in which the West Port was situated. That was the name of a narrow alley running into the Grassmarket, and it had come into notoriety in the early part of the century as the place in which was the house where Burke and Hare perpetrated those diabolical murders which gave a new verb—to burke—to the English language. The plan of Chalmers was to select a district of manageable compass, to cover it with volunteer workers from the churches, to have it thoroughly explored, and to have every individual in it personally invited to come to hear the preaching of the Gospel in a church close at hand. He found a tanner's loft, which he rented for a hall, and there himself commenced preaching operations. The issue was the building of a church, the setting of a pastor over it, and the gathering in of numbers of the most depraved and outcast of the population. Nor that alone, for now the example has been followed in many of the largest cities of Great Britain, and wherever the experiment has been wisely and perseveringly carried out, it has been attended with success. Dr. Chalmers never seems to me so great as when I think of him standing in that tanner's hall preaching to the people who came thither in their common attire to hear the Gospel from his lips. And I can understand the gusto with which he used to tell how one of his visitors, on entering into the room of a poor woman, and asking if she ever went to church, received for answer, "Yes." Where? "Oh just to the tannery hall ower by—ane Chalmers preaches —I like to encourage him, puir body!"

Only a month before his death the first communion was observed in the new building, which had by that time been erected, and the following extract from a letter to Mr. Lennox, of New York, will better show the heart of the man on this subject than any words of mine: "I wish to commemorate what to me is the most joyful event of my life. I have been intent for thirty years on the completion of a territorial experiment, and I have now to bless God for the consummation of it. Our church was opened on the 19th of February, and in one month my anxieties respecting an attendance have been set at rest. Five-sixths of the sittings have been let; but the best part of it is that three-fourths of these are from the West Port, a locality which two years ago had not one in ten church-goers from the whole population. I presided myself on Sabbath last over its first sacrament. There were one hundred and thirty-two communicants, and one hundred of them from the West Port."[*] On the day after that first communion he wrote to Mr. Tasker, the West Port pastor: "I have got now the desire of my heart—the church is finished, the schools are flourishing, our ecclesiastical machinery is about complete, and all in good working order. God has, indeed, heard my prayer, and I could now lay down my head in peace and die."

And indeed the end was near. In the month of

---

[*] Hanna's "Memoir of Life and Writings of Chalmers," vol. iv. p. 404.

May following he had been up in London giving testimony before a Committee of the House of Commons, and had returned to his home, when, on the morning of the 31st, the day on which he was expected to give before the Assembly the report of the College Committee, it was announced that he had died during the night, apparently in his sleep and without so much of a struggle as to disarrange in the least the drapery of his couch.

> "Servant of God, well done!
>   Rest from thy loved employ;
> The battle fought, the victory won,
>   Enter thy Master's joy.
>
> "The voice at midnight came:
>   He started up to hear;
> A mortal arrow pierced his frame,
>   He fell, but felt no fear.
>
> "Tranquil amidst alarms,
>   It found him in the field,
> A veteran slumbering on his arms
>   Beneath his red-cross shield.
>
> "His sword was in his hand,
>   Still warm with recent fight,
> Ready that moment at command
>   Through rock and steel to smite.
>
> "His spirit with a bound
>   Burst its encumbering clay;
> His tent at sunrise on the ground
>   A darkened ruin lay."

THOMAS CHALMERS.

There was in the mind of Chalmers a wonderful equipoise of opposites. With great mathematical ability there was combined keen metaphysical acumen, so that he was both a man of science and a mental philosopher. He was at home in political economy, but his hearty sympathies with his fellow-men, not to speak of his Christian love for all men, kept it in him from being the "Dismal Science" which it was to Thomas Carlyle. Grasping the greatest principles, he was at the same time alive to the importance of the minutest details. With the glowing imagination of the poet, he had all the practical sagacity of the wisest of his countrymen, and with the unwavering confidence of a great man, he had the simplicity—I had almost said the unconsciousness—of a little child. These qualities, so finely balanced, were all sublimed by genius, and heated to a constant incandescence by the consecrating influence of the Holy Spirit.

In person he was stout and almost stocky. His countenance when in repose was mild, his eye watery, almost dull, with a far-off look in it, as if he were gazing on things invisible to others, but when he became excited it lighted up as if with celestial fire, and shone with the lustre of genius. His speech betrayed him everywhere. It was not merely Scottish, but it was roughly provincial, and withal he read his discourses closely. Yet over all these disadvantages the force of the orator triumphed, so that even the cool, critical Jeffrey said of his eloquence that "it reminded him more of what one reads of as the effect of the eloquence of Demosthenes than anything he ever saw;" and again, that " he could not believe more had ever been done by the oratory of Demosthenes, Cicero, Burke, or Sheridan." To me it seems as if the force of his speech were due not merely to the qualities which I have enumerated, but also to two characteristics which he possessed in an almost unparalleled degree, and which enabled him to make use of all these others in any circumstances and at all times. The first of these was his power of abstraction. No matter where he was, he could withdraw himself from surrounding occurrences, and apply himself to the matter which he had in hand. Some of the sermons which, according to the critics, smelled so much of the lamp were written by snatches on his journeyings, in inns, and in the houses of his friends. It seemed as if at will he could withdraw into an inner chamber of his soul, where he could defy all interruption, and follow out the theme on which he was engaged.

Then, akin to that abstraction, and along with it, he had the power of concentration. Whatever he was prosecuting, he was for the time " totus in illo." His motto always might have been " This one thing I do." Whatever he took up with he could separate from all other things, and he could concentrate himself upon it. If it were mathematics, he was for the time exclusively devoted to that; if it were church extension, he gave himself wholly to that; if it were territorial missions, he saw nothing but them ; and so, being the man he otherwise was, he achieved great things in every department upon which he entered.

But it was in his sermons that the qualities of which I have spoken wrought the most remarkable results, for he saw only one thing in his text, and he devoted his discourse entirely to the enforcement of that. Robert Hall complained of him that he made no progress as he went on, but that he kept continually reproducing the same truth, only with added intensity of utterance and exuberance of illustration. But that was owing to the nature of the man. Other preachers seek to make different impressions in different portions of their sermons. Chalmers was content to make no more than one by the whole sermon : but when he had made that, it was indelible. No man who ever heard him could help seeing what he would be at, or could ever forget the importance which he gave it. His iterations and reiterations and re-reiterations were but like the whirlings of the sling from which at length the stone was sent whizzing to its mark; or like the gyrations of the eagle as it circles round and round in order only the more unerringly to swoop down upon its prey. His style was not meant for the eye, and so one soon tires of reading him; but for the ear it was most effective; and wherever, to this day, you meet with one who was privileged to listen to him from the pulpit, you will be sure to find him repeating to you the essence of the sermon which the great orator had distilled into a phrase that could not be misunderstood, and that would not allow itself to be forgotten.

Andrew Fuller visited him shortly after his conversion, and subsequently wrote thus to him: "After parting with you, I was struck with the importance which may attach to a single mind receiving an evangelical impression;" and the life whose course I have so imperfectly traced is an admirable illustration of the sagacity of that remark as applied to Chalmers. But when the same eminent divine, bewailing what he regarded as Chalmers's slavery to the manuscript, said, "If that man would but throw away his papers in the pulpit, he might be King of Scotland," he was not quite so accurate, for Chalmers kept his papers, and yet became the King of Scotland. But, as the old Scotch woman said, "It was fell readin' thon," and the earnestness of the man went through his "papers" into the souls of his hearers. Every man must do in that matter what he can do best, and it is not the mere presence of the papers, but what is on them, and what is behind them, that must determine whether they shall be a help or a hindrance.

It has been a life-long regret to me that, though I was eighteen years of age when Chalmers died, I never had the privilege of looking on his face, so leonine and yet so loving, or listening to his voice. I cannot, therefore, describe him to you as from personal observation; but as the best of many delineations of his appearance and eloquence in the pulpit which I have seen, I ask your indulgence while I read to you that of John Brown, M.D., the delightful author of "Rab and his Friends." It is taken from the second volume of his "Horæ Subsecivæ":

"We remember well our first hearing Dr. Chalmers. We were in a moorland district in Tweeddale, rejoicing in the country after nine months of the High School. We heard that the famous preacher was to be at a neighbouring parish church, and off we set, a cartful of irrepressible youngsters. 'Calm was all nature as a resting wheel.' The crows, instead of making wing, were impudent and still; the cart-horses, without knowing why, were standing, knowing the day, at the field gates, gossipping and gazing, idle and happy; the moor was stretching away in the pale sunlight—vast, dim, melancholy, like a sea; everywhere were to be seen the gathering people, 'springlings of blythe company;' the country-side seemed moved to one centre. As we entered the kirk we saw a notorious character, a drover, who had much of the brutal look of what he worked in, with the knowing eye of a man of the city—a sort of big Peter Bell.

> "'He had hardness in his eye,
> He had a hardness in his cheek.'

He was our terror, and we not only wondered but were afraid when we saw *him* going in. The kirk was as full as it could hold. How different it looks to a brisk town congregation! There was a fine leisureliness and vague stare; all the dignity and vacancy of animals; eyebrows raised and mouths open, as is the habit with those who speak little and look much, and at far-off objects. The minister comes in, homely in his dress and gait, but having a great look about him, 'like a mountain among hills.' The High School boys thought him like ' a big one of ourselves.' He looks vaguely round upon his audience, as if he saw in it *one great object*, *not many*. We shall never forget his smile—its general benignity; how he let the light of his countenance fall on us! He read a few verses quietly; then prayed briefly, solemnly, with his eyes wide open all the time, but not seeing. Then he gave out his text; we forget it, but its subject was 'Death reigns.' He stated slowly, calmly, the simple meaning of the words: what death was, and how and why it reigned; then suddenly he started and looked like a man who had seen some great sight, and was breathless to declare it. He told us how death reigned—everywhere, at all times, in all places; how we all knew it, how we would yet know more of it. The drover, who had sat down in the table-seat [square pew] opposite, was gazing up in a state of stupid excitement; he seemed restless, but never kept his eye from the speaker. The tide set in; everything added to its power; deep called to deep, imagery and illustration poured in, and every now and then the theme

—the simple, terrible statement—was repeated in some lucid interval. After overwhelming us with proofs of the reign of death, and transferring to us his intense urgency and emotion, and after shrieking, as if in despair, these words, '*Death is a tremendous necessity!*' he suddenly looked beyond, as if into some distant region, and cried out, 'Behold! a mightier! Who is this? He cometh from Edom, with dyed garments from Bozrah, glorious in his apparel, speaking in righteousness, travelling in the greatness of his strength, mighty to save.' Then in a few plain sentences he stated the truth as to sin entering, and death by sin, and death passing upon all. Then he took fire once more, and enforced with redoubled energy and richness the freeness, the simplicity, the security, the sufficiency of the great method of justification. How astonished and impressed we all were! He was at the full thunder of his power; the whole man was in an agony of earnestness. The drover was weeping like a child, the tears running down his ruddy, coarse cheeks, his face opened out and smoothed like an infant's, his whole body stirred with emotion. We had all insensibly been drawn out of our seats, and were converging towards the wonderful speaker; and when he sat down, after warning each one of us to remember who it was and what it was that followed Death on the pale horse, and how alone we could escape, we all sank back into our seats. How beautiful to our eyes did the thunderer look!—exhausted, but sweet and pure. How he poured out his soul before his God in giving thanks for sending the Abolisher of Death! Then a short psalm, and all was ended.

"We went home quieter than we came. We did not recount the foals, with their long legs and roguish eyes, and their sedate mothers; we did not speculate upon whose dog *that* was, and whether that was a crow or a man in the dim moor. We thought of other things—that voice, that face, those great, simple, living thoughts, those floods of resistless eloquence, that piercing, shattering voice, that ' tremendous necessity.' "

One knows not whether to admire more the description or the thing described; but one thing is clear, the eloquence which inspired that description, even after the lapse of the years between boyhood and middle life, must have been eloquence indeed, combining in itself the force of the torrent and the fulness of the sea.

VII.

THE PULPITS OF THE DISSENTING CHURCHES.

For the sake of clearness and continuity, we have thus far confined ourselves almost entirely to the pulpit of the Scottish Church as by law established; but now, in bringing these sketches to a close, we must devote a little attention to the representative preachers of the Dissenting denominations.

Of the smaller bodies, the oldest was that known in recent years as the Reformed Presbyterian Church. It represented the "Society Men," or "Covenanters," who never really joined the Church of the Revolution settlement, because it had not insisted on everything that was required in the National Covenant and the Solemn League. For a considerable time this honourable remnant had no ordained ministers, but as the years went on it grew in numbers and in strength, though it never became large, and finally, about fourteen or fifteen years ago, it united, all but a very small minority, with the Free Church. But its record was excellent, and one at least of its ministers deserves a high place among the great preachers of Scotland.

Dr. WILLIAM SYMINGTON, born at Paisley in 1795, and educated at the University of Glasgow and the Theological Seminary of the Reformed Presbyterian Church, was ordained at Stranraer in 1819, and transferred to Glasgow in 1838, where he laboured till his death in 1862. He was a man of magnificent presence, fine culture, exquisite taste, great strength of mind, and admirable common-sense. While faithfully attending to his pastoral work, he was a diligent student, and his sermons were all carefully prepared. Clear in his style, logical in his arrangement, elegant and impressive in his delivery, he drew around him men of intelligence and weight of character, and he had an influence far beyond the limits of the small denomination of which he was an ornament. His works on "The Atonement and Intercession of Jesus Christ," on "The Mediatorial Dominion of Jesus Christ," and on "Messiah the Prince," some of which have been reprinted in this country, are still valued by students of systematic theology; and his courses of monthly evening lectures on such subjects as the history of Joseph and the Book of Daniel are still remembered for their eloquence and power by multitudes who heard them from his lips. His method of preparing these last is thus described by one of his sons: "They were the fruit of much careful premeditation —not fully written out, much less read, but thoroughly studied and digested, the beginning of each sentence and references to texts being put down in neat and orderly form. Not read, certainly, for no one understood more thoroughly the true theory of preaching as a *concio ad populum*— an address in which the speaker is in full electric communication with his hearers. The larger writing was reduced to notes on a thin slip. These he went over again and again until his mind was familiar with the whole process of thought; by prayer his soul was brought up to the level of the Divine message he was charged to utter, and thus were secured the pellucid clearness, the obvious mastery, the unaffected unction which made his preaching so attractive and so useful."*

---

* Biographical sketch prefixed to "Messiah the Prince." 1881.

His name may not be so familiar to you on this side of the Atlantic as those of others in the larger denominations; but in a day when the pulpits of Glasgow were filled by some of the ablest men of their time, he was the equal, and in one or two respects perhaps the superior, of them all. He was remarkable above most for the combination of manliness with grace which appeared both in his thinking and in his manner; and if he had been in the Established Church he would most assuredly have taken a place among the foremost leaders on the side of spiritual independence.

Another of these smaller denominations was the Original Secession Church. I need not go into the history of its formation; indeed I am not sure that I could give it with entire accuracy in every particular; but it was connected with some difference of opinion between the members of one branch of the Seceders in regard to the principle of a State Church. None of them, in practice, were State Churchmen, but some of them, in theory, maintained that the ideal Church was a State Church, while others repudiated State Churchism as altogether and everywhere pernicious, and that led to a separation. Of this little denomination of theoretical State Churchmen, the great man—and he was a great man—was Dr. THOMAS MCCRIE, the famous biographer of John Knox. Born at Duns in 1772, educated at the University of Edinburgh and the Theological Seminary of the Anti-Burghers, he was ordained at Edinburgh in 1796, and laboured in that city till his death, in 1835. Though his forte was historical investigation, of which his works on the Reformation in Italy and Spain, as well as his biographies of Knox and Melville, were the rich fruits, yet he was no mean preacher. A volume of his sermons is preserved in the collected edition of his works, and, like the man, they are weighty and solid, somewhat heavy in style, but always luminous, and invariably Jesus is in the midst. His lectures on Esther are among the finest specimens of the best sort of practical exposition of the historical portions of the Scriptures; and, together with Peddie's Jonah and Dick's lectures on the Acts of the Apostles, they may be regarded as models for that class of discourses. McCrie had a singular charm for Hugh Miller, who in his early stonemason days was a frequent attendant on his ministry, and who has left a delightful sketch of him in his miscellaneous works. I extract the following sentences: "We were struck by the great simplicity of his manner and style, and listened rather soothed and pleased by his lucid statements of important truths, grounded, if we may so express ourselves, on a deep substratum of serious feeling, than surprised by any marked originality of view. By-and-by, however, when the first obvious principles were laid down, he began to draw inferences. Ah! thought we, as we sat up erect in the pew, there now is something we never heard before. The discourse, simple and quiet at its commencement, had assumed a new character. The unquestioned but common truths were but the foundations of the edifice. . . . . There were remarks on human nature that from their graphic shrewdness reminded us of Crabbe, and yet the mode was entirely different. There were gleams of fancy that, falling for a moment on some of the remoter recesses of the subject, lighted them up into sudden brightness, and when fully shown the gleam disappeared. There were strokes of eloquence, condensed at times into a single sentence, that found their way direct to the heart, and far conclusions attained by a few steps through vistas of thought unopened before." * This is high praise coming

---

* "Headship of Christ," p. 97 : Hugh Miller.

from such a quarter, and the reader of McCrie's sermons will have to confess that it is not exaggerated.

Coming now to the United Secession Church, and seeking in it mainly for epoch-marking men, I mention first JOHN BROWN, D.D., of Edinburgh. There were great and good preachers in both branches of the Secession before his day, but their style was patterned largely after that of the Erskines and the Marrow men. Their discourses were systematic in form, after a stereotyped method, and, unless in exceptional cases, without much beauty of style or felicity of illustration, or any pretension to exegetical exactness. But in the last of these particulars the name of John Brown marks the beginning of an era not only in his own denomination, but in Scotland generally. He was in that country very much what Moses Stuart was in New England—the regenerator, if not the father, of exact Scriptural exegesis, and for that he deserves to be held in lasting honour. Born at Whitburn in 1784, and educated at the University of Edinburgh and the Theological Seminary of the Burghers, he was ordained at Biggar in 1806, and removed to Edinburgh in 1822, where he continued till his death, in 1858. He was the third in direct succession of what his son has called the "dynasty" of the Browns. His grandfather was the famous John Brown of Haddington, the author of the "Self-Interpreting Bible," and the venerable man of whom David Hume said that he preached as if the Lord Jesus Christ were at his elbow. His father was John Brown of Whitburn, a simple-hearted man, without any striking mental qualities, whose goodness was his greatness, and who was an effective preacher as well as an earnest Evangelist. His son was John Brown, M.D., *facile princeps* the most delightful essayist of his age.

The theological instructor of Dr. Brown was Dr. George Lawson of Selkirk, a man of great learning, profound sagacity, and catholic spirit, whose lectures on Ruth, Joseph, Esther, and "The Book of Proverbs" are still worthy of study, and whose influence as a professor in moulding the ministry of his denomination for more than twenty years cannot well be over-estimated. His students, some of whom I met in my earlier days as venerable old men, all but worshipped his memory, and the impression produced by him on John Brown was seen in many ways, but principally in the ultimate tendency of his mind to critical studies, in the desire which he evinced to simplify the style of theology and go back from human systems to Scripture, in the prominence given by him to moral teaching as an integral part of the Gospel, and in his liberal views as to Christian forbearance and the freedom of the Church from secular control.

His gifted son has told us, in that admirable letter to Dr. Cairns which is the gem of his works, how Dr. Brown came, after his great and crushing bereavement, to " take up with" Vitringa and other German expositors; and the studies thus commenced in Biggar were continued in Edinburgh, where for more than twenty years he combined the work of a professorship of theology with that of the pastorate. Even before he entered on his professorship, however, he had instituted for the students attending his congregation, and such others as chose to be present with them, a weekly class for the study of the Greek New Testament—and among these early pupils were William Cunningham, afterwards Principal of the Free Church College, and David Brown, the commentator on the first six books of the New Testament, in the well-known work by Jamieson, Fausset, and Brown, and quite recently the Moderator of the Free Church.

As a preacher, Dr. Brown's power lay in the clear

statement and cogent enforcement of the meaning of the Scriptures. His great aim seemed to be to bring his hearers face to face with the Word, and to make them feel that they had to do with God as its author. But to do that he had to make very clear what the Scriptures really said, and to discover that he brought all the resources at his command to bear upon the investigation of the portion which he had in hand. His Expository Discourses were perhaps a little too learned for the pulpit, and a little too popular for the professor's chair—a thing almost inevitable from the fact that they had to pay a double debt by doing duty in both; but they were always clear, honest, independent, and for the most part satisfactory. He never needed any one to interpret his meaning, and he shrank with his whole soul from handling the Word of God deceitfully. A very common formula with him was this: "*That* is truth, and very important truth, but it is not the truth taught in this passage." He did not interpret the Bible so as to make it suit his system, but he modified his system so as to harmonize it with the Scriptures; and no matter how many authorities might be ranged on either side of a controverted interpretation, he would judge for himself, and take that which for good and satisfactory reasons commended itself to his own acceptance. His discourses now may seem to be in some degree superseded by the labours of later commentators, who are better furnished for their work than it was possible for him then to be; but the impulse given to that general forward movement in exegetical theology by which he has himself been somewhat superseded, came first and mainly from himself, and, remembering my own obligations to him, it is with peculiar veneration and affectionate gratitude that I have dwelt thus upon his work. When I sat at his feet he seemed to me to be one of the finest-looking men I had ever seen. His face was beautifully chiselled, almost like marble; his forehead was high and bare; his thin white locks flowed lengthily over his ears and collar; his eye was black and piercing, like an eagle's—it seemed as if it were looking you through; and his voice was clear and ringing, sometimes trumpet-like. He read closely, and as his writing—very foolishly, as I think—was almost microscopic in its neat minuteness, he had to bend very low over his manuscript. But even with all these disadvantages, his reading, as his son has said, was "a fine and high art, or rather gift," and when he was thoroughly roused the effect was great.

But exposition was his passion, and it was

scarcely possible to be a member of his class without catching the infection of his enthusiasm. He had little of the gift of insight or of the faculty of imagination, but he made up largely for the want of these by indomitable industry, and it was said that one could not live a month under his roof without learning to be a student. Later writers have developed his principles further than he could carry them, but his works will remain a noble monument to the industry, no less than to the reverence, with which he studied the Word of God.

The revival of exegetical study inaugurated by John Brown was carried a long way forward by JOHN EADIE, a minister of the same denomination, and for more than thirty years a professor in the same theological seminary. Born at Alva in 1810, he studied at the University of Glasgow, and was ordained to the ministry in that city in 1835. He was appointed to the Professorship of Biblical Literature in 1843, and held both offices until his death, in 1876. It was my privilege to be a member of his congregation during my student life in Glasgow, to attend his classes in the Theological Seminary, and, in later days, to know him as a friend and counsellor. He was never a "popular" preacher, in the current sense of that phrase. His manner was not elegant. His utterance was thick, and there was in it an occasional " click," like that which characterizes certain South African languages. There was nothing of the showy or sensational about him. The first time you heard him you were struck with the clear, fresh, striking explanation which he gave of some passage which had heretofore been obscure to you, but you were not at all attracted by his elocution. You went again, however, and this time you saw less that was objectionable and heard more that was satisfying, and so it went on, week by week, until you could not persuade yourself to go elsewhere. I never heard him without having something added to my stock of knowledge, or some difficulty removed out of my mind, or some new interest given to some particular portion of the Word of God. He had the habit of reading in the morning service consecutively through some book of the Bible, and of commenting on the portion read in a brief and simple manner. I had the privilege of hearing him thus go over the larger part of the prophecies of Isaiah, and though his comment was thrown into the service as a kind of extra—for it was followed after singing with a discourse proper—it was so truly a feast of fat things that it would have been worth going a long way to hear, even if there had been nothing more. He had great versatility, and, with the exception of mathematics, he intermeddled with all knowledge. He read voraciously. His memory was so retentive that he forgot nothing, and so ready that he could always recall that which he wanted. His scholarship was perhaps more extensive in area than accurate in detail, although even in the latter respect he was all the time improving; so that at length, without having the advantages, earlier and later, of these English dignitaries, he was the worthy compeer of Alford and Ellicott, even in the departments in which they are acknowledged masters. His commentaries differ from most other exegetical works in the glow of unction by which they are pervaded; a quality which is, perhaps, to be traced to the fact that while he was preparing them for the press in the study, he was also, at the same time, engaged in the public exposition of the same books in the pulpit. Latterly he did not write his discourses fully out, but, like Elihu, he was always "full of matter," and seemed to be "refreshed by speaking." His industry was prodigious, and by a careful disposition of his time he was able to carry on the work of his pastorate most efficiently even while he was enriching his brethren with his learned expositions. He had the advantage of Dr. Brown in his familiarity with the German language and in the possession of a rich imagination, but he lacked the forceful utterance of his venerable colleague, and he rarely if ever became impassioned; but along with James Morison—also a pupil of John Brown, and whose commentaries on Matthew, Mark, and the third chapter of the Epistle to the Romans are unsurpassed by any in the English language—he helped to keep Scotland abreast of other lands in the important department of Scripture exegesis.

But perhaps, as regards pulpit efficiency, in all the comprehensiveness of that phrase, the man who did most to modernize and to energize the preaching of the Secession Church was DAVID KING, whose biography has been recently issued from the press. Born at Montrose in 1806, and educated partly at Aberdeen and partly at Edinburgh, he was ordained at Dalkeith in 1830, and transferred to Glasgow in 1833, where he held one of the foremost places among its preachers for twenty years. Then came a break-down in health, from which he never fully rallied, for after brief pastorates in London and Edinburgh he retired into private life, and died in 1883. He was an admirable organizer, and made his Glasgow church a model in this regard to all around. He was intensely public-spirited, and took an active part upon the platform in all efforts for liberty and benevolence. He managed also to find time for scientific investigation, so that he became an authority in all questions affecting the relations of modern discovery to theology. But the pulpit was with him supreme. Every Lord's Day was to him a great occasion, and he always endeavoured to serve God with his best. In the words of another: "One might say he inaugurated a new era in the preaching of the Seceders. Before that it had been mainly theological, ... abounding in well-worn phrases and distinctions, earnest no doubt, but as a whole in a somewhat cumbrous, conventional, and formal style, scarcely ever losing sight of certain safeguards and subtleties. Dr. King, certainly not alone, but in a prominent and powerful way, put the breath of modern life and thought through this. He had a strong philosophical tendency. He was eloquent, imaginative, polished, and classic in style, and, beyond all question, intense. He was among the first of our preachers of any sort who had the modern attraction of shortness." * His discourses were delivered at

---

* "Memoir and Sermons of Dr. David King," pp. 45, 46.

first without notes, but latterly he used a manuscript, *through* which, rather than *from* which, he gave his thoughts to the people. His sermons were remarkable for their climatic structure, rising from stage to stage, as one has beautifully said, " like a succession of terraces in an Alpine road," and at each turning the great theme stood forth before you in new freshness and interest. Students of all denominations were attracted to his congregation, and his influence went far beyond the limits of his own church, and is felt to this hour in the hearts of many who are still preaching the Gospel in his native land.

The preaching of the ministers in the Relief branch of the United Presbyterian Church was different from that of those in all the other denominations. I have failed to find an explanation of the fact, but it is certain that it was rhetorical, ornate, almost florid, alike in matter and in manner. These preachers did not hide the truth by any means. They were thoroughly Evangelical. They preached Christ in all the comprehensiveness of the apostolic sense of these words, but they did so in a style which sometimes tended to divert attention from the subject to the manner. They seem to have formed themselves after the great French preachers more than any others. They wrote their discourses with great care, committed them to memory with infinite pains, and practised elocution with great success. Such a discipline as that of Bourdaloue, described by Bungener in "The Preacher and the King," represents the sort of training to which, I judge, they must have subjected themselves, and the result was seen in the immense popularity attained by some of them whose names, quite unknown on this side of the sea, are now all but forgotten in their own land.* But they were more than mere rhetoricians, for they did effective service in the land. They deserve to be held in honour, not only for their proclamation of the truth as it is in Jesus, but also because they were the first in Scotland to welcome Christians as such, irrespective of denominational differences, to the fellowship of the Lord's Supper with them, and because, wherever there was a wrong to be redressed, or a right to be

---

* Thus it is told of a young man, the Rev. Mr. Struthers, of South College Street Church, Edinburgh, that during his brief ministry there the young "advocates" of the Parliament House flocked to his ministrations just to study his elocution.

maintained, or an abuse to be condemned, they were invariably in the front.

The man of most mark among them—not because he represented them in the rhetorical peculiarity which I have just specified, but for his genius and distinctive individuality, amounting even to eccentricity—was Dr. WILLIAM ANDERSON. Born at Kilsyth in 1799, and educated at the University of Glasgow, he was licensed to preach in 1820, and shortly after, was called to the pastorate of John Street Church, Glasgow, in which he continued till his death, in 1872. His ordination was delayed for upwards of a year, because of a controversy which arose between him and the Presbytery. He had quoted Shakespeare in the pulpit (!), and above all, and worse than all, he read his sermons; therefore the Presbytery refused to ordain him unless he promised to give up these practices. But although he was then only in his twenty-second year, he firmly withstood that demand, and after a while the Presbytery yielded. As a preacher Anderson was, before all other things, Evangelical, but he was not, therefore, common-place. His discourses were marked by originality of thought, raciness of illustration, and fervour of appeal. They brought the

Gospel to bear on the experiences of everyday life, and on the great questions which happened to be at the moment before the public mind. He stood always at the foot of the Cross, but from that centre he swept the circumference of active life, and discussed the first Reform Bill, the emancipation of the slaves, the iniquity of the Corn Laws, the condition of the masses, and the controversies between capital and labour. Indeed, whatever "the present truth" might be, one was very sure to hear some ringing and suggestive utterance upon it from the John Street pulpit. More than any other man in Scotland he vindicated the liberty of the pulpit to deal with any subject that concerned the welfare of humanity. The cannon mounted on his battery was no fixture which could be fired only through one embrasure, but, like the turret-gun of an ironclad, it could sweep the whole horizon, and could be brought to bear on the enemies of truth and liberty wherever they were. He was not afraid, either, to make use of humour in his sermons. He had a quaint way of putting things, which was often heightened by his mode of snuff-taking, a habit to which he was greatly addicted. After uttering some of his cutting sarcasms or pungent reproofs, he would bring his finger and thumb, with the

PULPITS OF DISSENTING CHURCHES.

naughty dust between them, from his vest-pocket, and convey it to his nostril with a sniff which could express at will either contempt or scorn or triumph, so that it was amusing to see how he could turn an act in itself disagreeable to excellent oratorical account. Two volumes of his sermons have been published, and there is not a discourse in either volume which is not in some way remarkable; but his ablest production—I consider it, indeed, the greatest book on the subject in our language— is his treatise on Regeneration. It has been republished in this country, and is very dear to me because of the comfort and guidance which it brought me at a critical time in my own history. Possibly I am for that reason prone to exaggerate its merits, but I very earnestly commend it to your studious perusal.

Passing now to the Congregationalists, a word ought to be said in honour of DAVID RUSSELL, of Dundee, whose treatise on Infant Salvation was the earliest presentation of what is now the common faith on that subject which Scotland produced. Its publication almost of itself brought round the Christian opinion of the land to its conclusions, and broadened out "elect infants" into all children dying in infancy. That was a service to theology too signal to be quite overlooked.

But the two men whose names as preachers stand highest among Scottish Congregationalists were RALPH WARDLAW and WILLIAM LINDSAY ALEXANDER. Wardlaw was born at Dalkeith in 1779, was educated at the University of Glasgow and at the Theological Seminary of the Burgher denomination, then under the charge of Dr. Lawson, of Selkirk; but becoming convinced of the Scripturalness of Congregational independency, he publicly identified himself at the end of his theological course with the Congregational body, and was ultimately ordained over the newly formed North Albion Street Church, Glasgow, in 1803. With that city his name and ministry are thoroughly identified, and for a period of fifty years, up till his death in 1853, he was one of the foremost citizens and one of the ablest preachers in the western capital of Scotland. He was in his last decade before I had the privilege of looking on his face or listening to his words, and much of the vigour of his earlier days had gone, but there were still the calm dignity, the clear style, the logical cogency, the judicial candour, and the acute analytical power for which all through life he was remarkable. He had never much of the impassioned, and rarely became animated or intense, but his reading was exquisitely beautiful, and it was a delight to hear him preach.

It was his lot throughout his public life to appear very frequently as a controversialist. He did good service in that way by his writings on the Socinian, the Baptist, the Voluntary, and other discussions of his day, and one of the latest works which came from his pen was a vindication of Congregationalism. His contest was never so much for victory as for truth, and his spirit was always that of charity. He never reasoned disingenuously, or sought to make an argument carry more weight than it could honestly bear. He never mistook a bad name for good argument. He never imputed unworthy motives to his antagonists, and he took good care always to put their case as accurately and as strongly as it could be stated. He was emphatically a Christian gentleman, and though often sorely provoked, he never allowed his temper to affect his pen. The result was that, without giving unnecessary pain to his adversaries, his writings were all the more powerful with the public jury to whom they were addressed; and often, in times of strife and debate, when the *odium theologicum* is running high, I have wished that the combatants on both sides had come under the influence of Wardlaw in these respects.

His pulpit method is thus described by his biographer: " It was his habit in the early period of his ministry to deliver his discourses from memory after he had written them fully and carefully out; or from meditation, after having put down in writing an outline of what he meant to say, the latter being by much the more frequent plan with him. Discourses so delivered were probably wanting in that minute accuracy and grace of expression which characterized his later compositions after he adopted the plan of reading whatever he uttered from the pulpit; but I have heard those who were in the habit of listening to him at this time express their regret at the absence from his later discourses of that pungency and animation which his earlier discourses seldom wanted."* One worthy member of his congregation said that for long after he began to " use the paper " he always felt ready to cry out the words of the Lord regarding Lazarus—" Loose him and let him go." But when he adopted the manuscript, the care which he took to become a *good* reader, and the advantage which he possessed in

---

* "Life of Wardlaw," p. 77: W. L. Alexander, D.D., LL.D.

a naturally musical voice and carefully modulated enunciation, tended to overcome prejudice, and made his reading ultimately perhaps more acceptable than his free speech had been. In the forenoon service he generally gave himself to exposition, and his works on the Proverbs, Ecclesiastes, the Prophecies of Zechariah, the Epistle to the Romans, and the Epistle of James, are the evidences of his diligence and ability in that particular department. There was little of what could be termed genius about him, but he had a strength and beauty of his own. His strength lay in the critical and ratiocinative faculties, and his beauty came from his exact and elegant taste. His sense of the becoming was rarely, if ever, at fault, and his appreciation of the beautiful, whether in nature or sentiment, was quick and just. He had also a playful wit, but that he kept rigidly out of the pulpit, reserving it entirely for moments of social intercourse, and even then never allowing it to trespass beyond the limits of propriety. His biography, by Dr. Alexander, is one of the most instructive books of its class, combining in itself almost a course of theology and a treatise on homiletics. It gives not only the outline of Dr. Wardlaw's works, but also Dr. Alexander's criticisms on them, so that we have the best of both men on the subjects treated. The course thus followed by Dr. Alexander was severely commented on by many, but the spirit in which his criticisms were made, and the value of the criticisms themselves, give a permanent importance to the book, which I very earnestly commend to your attention.

But we must say a few emphatic words concerning WILLIAM LINDSAY ALEXANDER himself. Born at Leith, on the 24th of August 1808, he was educated at schools there and in East Linton, and after three years at the University of Edinburgh he went for two years to the University of St. Andrews, where he came under the influence of Dr. Chalmers, for whom, throughout his life, he cherished the greatest affection and admiration. After a brief attendance at the Theological Academy of the Congregationalists, in Glasgow, he was called to the Classical Tutorship of the Independent College, Blackburn, England. From this, with a brief interval, during which he made trial of his preaching gifts in sundry places, he passed to Liverpool, where for a year and a half he supplied the pulpit of Newington Chapel. His ministry in Edinburgh began on January 1, 1835, and there, first in the Argyle Square Chapel and afterwards in Augustine Church, which he was himself instrumental in erecting, and which he named after the Christian Father who of all others was held by him in highest veneration, he ministered till within a year of his death, in 1884. He was a ripe scholar, especially in Greek and Hebrew; his attainments in the former enabling him to rank with the best Grecians of the day, and his eminence in the latter securing him a place in the Old Testament Company of the Westminster Revisers. His works are numerous and weighty, and by his editorship of the best edition of Kitto's Cyclopædia he has laid all Bible students under heavy obligation. His industry was unflagging. He had no faith in pastoral visitation, and little aptitude for it, hence he left that to others; but he was diligent at his desk, and in the pulpit he always fed his people with the finest of the wheat. I recall him as he was in those days, now nearly forty years ago, when, during my seminary course, I was regularly to be found in his morning audience. He preached then in the old Argyle Chapel, to a congregation more remarkable for weight of character than for numbers. As he took his place in the pulpit, one could not but be struck with the breadth and loftiness of his lordly brow and the firm expression of his mobile mouth. As he looked abroad upon his audience you marked also the keen searching glance of his eyes; but when he began the service, you forgot everything else in the devotional absorption into which, whether you would or not, you were withdrawn by him. His prayers lifted the very petitions which you were wishing to present, and there was no misgiving in the " Amen " with which you responded. His sermons were generally on great subjects. One, I remember with a vivid distinctness, was on the Eternity of God; another, from the text, " Be sure your sin will find you out," burned indelibly into me the difference between the expressions " Your sin will be found out " and " Your sin will find out you." They were all remarkable for the weight of their thought, the clearness of their style, and the earnestness of their appeal. His pathos was a power. It never unmanned him, but it always affected you. And sometimes when he was roused, his indignant scorn of wrongdoing, or his withering sarcasm in the exposure of some specious infidel objection, was positively tremendous.*

---

* His sarcastic humour came out in these days very freely, and some very droll instances of it are related by his biographer in the admirable memoir recently issued. I give two others that were current among the students of my generation. One morning an unusual number of pulpit notices had been sent to him from all quarters to be read at the public service. The thing had become a nuisance, and he

In his later days some of these qualities were absent. and the mellowness of experience came in their stead to give a new charm to his addresses. I never heard him in a regular series of expositions through any one book, but indeed the groundwork of every sermon he preached was exposition; for the first thing he always did was to show the meaning of his text, and lift his subject naturally out of it.

---

wished to rebuke it. So, arranging the pile in such a manner as to make his act effective, he lifted them up, and let them fall in a long, fluttering series to his feet, saying the while, in his most withering style, "Do they mean to turn this pulpit—such as it is—into a column of the *North British Advertiser?*" The manner in which he alluded to the pulpit, which he used jokingly to call "the horse-box," and which was ugly enough in all conscience, was inimitably grotesque. He was not often troubled with a drowsy audience, but he could not tolerate a deliberate employment of the pew as a sleeping-place. One day, just as he was giving out his text, he saw a man in the front seat of the side gallery, almost within reach of him, carefully fold his arms upon the book-board and lay his head upon them, as if settling himself for a snooze. He could not let such an act pass unnoticed, and the way in which he reproved it was characteristic. He stood still and silent for what seemed quite a while, until the culprit, wondering what the matter was, raised his head a few inches and looked up. This was all the Doctor was waiting for, and, gracefully bowing to the offender, he said, "Good-night, my friend." Needless to say there was no sleep for him throughout that service.

He read his sermons from manuscript, but such was the hold he took of you from the first that you forgot in a few moments all about the "paper." Often, in the heat and intensity of his mental action, the discourse "boiled over" into extempore speech, and then you might expect some terse and pungent sayings. Sometimes, too, after he had shut the book, he lingered to say a few tender words or to make a last solemn appeal, beautiful in the calmness of its love, and bearing the same relation to the discourse as the motion of a vessel, after the engines have ceased their action, does to its propulsion by the screw. He was like an extra professor to me while I was at the United Presbyterian Seminary, and not unfrequently the great majority of my fellow-students were present in his congregation. In the brilliant galaxy of preachers who made Edinburgh famous during the fifth and sixth decades of this century he had a place distinctively his own, and they who heard his discourses wondered no less at their excellence than at the number and ability of his published works.

Reverting now to the Established Church since the date of the Disruption, I have room here for but the briefest mention of NORMAN MACLEOD.

After the departure of the Free Churchmen there was for a time a great scarcity of men of mark in the Establishment; and, as one of its leaders of to-day has remarked, " third-rate men were in several instances brought from the obscurity to which they were born, and in which they should have been allowed to die, to occupy prominent pulpits," * so that perhaps it was easier for one possessed of ability to find his way to the front than in other circumstances it might have been. But in any circumstances Norman Macleod would have become a leader. Born at Campbelton in 1812, he was educated mainly at the University of Glasgow, but went for two years in his theological course to Edinburgh, that he might enjoy the prelections of Chalmers. He was ordained to the ministry in Loudoun, Ayrshire, in 1838, was transferred to Dalkeith in 1843, and thence to the Barony parish, Glasgow, in 1851, where he laboured till his death, in 1872. In his early Loudoun days his form and features were familiar to me. I was then a boy at the Kilmarnock Academy, and he was one of the most popular of the neighbouring clergy who used to come to its annual examinations, for he was sure

* " Scottish Divines," Third Series, p. 393.

to request before he left that a special holiday should be given us because of the good appearance we had made. He was always an assistant at the communion in the parish church, and I have still a distinct recollection of hearing and enjoying his evening sermons on such occasions. His parish was only a few miles from my home, and the report of his successful effort to fill his church at a special evening service, with the people in their working garb, was told with a kind of wonderment, as something utterly unheard-of before, by the farmers of the district when they came to market. He was then distinctly Evangelical in his teachings, and whatever may be said of his opinions at a later day, he never lost the fervour of spirit by which, at that time, he was characterized.

But it was during his Barony pastorate that he came most prominently into view; and in that, splendid as in many other respects it was, nothing was so great as his work among the labouring classes, whom, after the plan which he had followed in Loudoun, he gathered into the house of God on the evening of the first day of the week in large numbers, and in their "white jackets," and multitudes of whom were admitted by him, after careful examination, to the membership of his church. He was a great, full-rounded, whole-souled *man*, and his thorough humanness was the substratum of his power. Add to that his joyous love of Nature, his Celtic temperament, with its poetic susceptibility and its occasional weird out-flashings of mystic might, his devotional fervour, which, to the surprise of so many—though Dr. Flint says it was no surprise to him—came out so fully in his diary, his deep well of tender sympathy with suffering, of which his " Wee Davie " may be taken as a specimen, and his intense desire to do good to all with whom he came into contact, and you have the qualities which were most distinctive in his character. The hackneyed words of Terence, " Homo sum ; humani nihil a me alienum puto," were exactly appropriate to him, and he could make himself equally at home in the palace of the Queen and in the workshop of a Newmilns weaver. In private he had a great fund of humour, some of it even rollicking in its heartiness, and a great wealth of anecdote ; and in the pulpit, when he was great he was great indeed. But he was, like all men of his temperament, unequal in his discourses. When he was " in full flood," however, he carried all before him. When he was in his prime, I rather think that he wrote his discourses fully out, and either delivered from memory or read from the manuscript, as suited him best on the occasion. But in his later days, while giving much premeditation to his sermon, he left himself free to take the language which came to him at the moment, so that he combined " the self-control of the prepared discourse with the directness of extemporaneous effort," and the address approached the conversational, which, in the estimation of some—though I confess that I am not one of them—is the true ideal of a sermon. Theologically he might be ranked with the English Broad Churchmen. He adopted the views of Macleod Campbell on the Atonement, those of Arnold on the Church, and, unless I have mistaken his meaning in some of his letters, those of the Restorationists on eschatology. How he reconciled the last of these with his acceptance of the Westminster Confession I am unable to say, and I fear that his influence has had much to do with the strengthening of that current which has set in towards the opinions advocated by some of the contributors to the volume of Scotch sermons which was published a few years ago. Undeniably, he never could have advocated such rationalistic doctrines as are to be found in one or two of these discourses, but his views on the significance of subscription to a creed may have encouraged their authors to put them forward.

In the Free Church, just subsequent to the Disruption, there was a group of remarkable men, who may be called the lieutenants of Chalmers, to at least two of whom, before we conclude, we must direct your attention. These two are ROBERT SMITH CANDLISH and THOMAS GUTHRIE. Candlish was born in Edinburgh in 1803, educated at the University of Glasgow, and after some years spent as an assistant, first in Glasgow and latterly in Bonhill, he was ordained to the ministry of St. George's, Edinburgh, in 1834, where, first in the Established and afterwards in the Free Church, he laboured till his death, in 1873. He was one of the great debaters in the Disruption controversy. His speeches were like trumpet-calls for the mustering of the hosts to battle, and "one blast upon his bugle-horn was worth ten thousand men." But it is mainly as a preacher that we must speak of him here. In personal appearance he was peculiar. I question if any one ever saw him for the first time without being tempted to smile. His body was diminutive, but what it lacked appeared to have been given to the head, which for size would not have sat amiss upon the shoulders of a giant. His hair hung all around it in tangled luxuriance, sometimes almost like a mop. His mouth was large, and the under-jaw slightly protuberant. His eyes were restless and flashing, and his forehead full. He went up the pulpit stair with a hurried step, and running his fingers through his hair, he gave out the psalm in a defiant tone, as if he meant to let some one know that he would not be put down. When he came to the sermon, he indulged unconsciously in all manner of convulsive movements, twisting and writhing like one in agony. He clutched at his gown, he took hold of the Bible as if he would lift it and throw it at his audience, he grasped the pulpit like one who feared he was about to fall. But all this while he had been opening up his text in a manner so clear, so comprehensive, so suggestive, that, as he proceeded, you forgot his eccentricities of manner, and felt only the power of his words. His forte was in exposition and practical appeal, and he was never so great as when he was engaged in the analysis of some Scripture character, and the enforcement of the lessons which it conveyed to modern times. Sometimes he was exceedingly subtle, and it was difficult to follow him, but in general the lines of his thought were well defined;

so that while his discourses were an intellectual treat to the most refined, they were also enjoyed by the plainest and least educated of the audience. He had none of the pictorial or illustrative power of Guthrie, but his appeals had a more searching character and a more incisive edge. He grappled at once with the intellect and the conscience, and made every one feel that he had to do with God. Listening to him at such a time was like being subjected to a sort of spiritual vivisection. Like Chalmers, he read his discourses, even to slavishness; but, as in the case of Chalmers, it was "fell reading." Sometimes he preached without a manuscript, but on such occasions he was very unequal, and in later years it was but rarely that he attempted that manner of address. He was an instance of a man pushing his way into the very front of pulpit orators, in spite of many positive blemishes, by the pure force of his intellectual pre-eminence, spiritual insight, and impassioned fervour, and there were not wanting many imitators who thought that they had clothed themselves in the strength of their model when they had succeeded only in putting on one of his weaknesses.

THOMAS GUTHRIE was not, like Candlish, a great debater and ecclesiastical statesman, but he was the popular orator, carrying all before him, not so much by the power of logic as by the appositeness of his illustrations, the force of his humour, and the depth of his pathos.

He was born at Brechin in 1803, and educated first at the schools of his native place, and afterwards at the University of Edinburgh. He was licensed to preach in 1825, but being disappointed in obtaining a parish, he went to Paris, where he studied medicine for a time. On his return to his native place he conducted a bank agency for two years, and at length, in 1830, he was ordained to the pastorate of Arbirlot. Thence he was translated to the collegiate charge of New Greyfriars, in Edinburgh, in 1837; and from that he was transferred to the parish of St. John's, in the same city, in 1840. After the Disruption he became minister of Free St. John's, which charge he held till 1864, when he became *pastor emeritus*. During the last years of his life he was editor of the *Sunday Magazine*, in the pages of which most of his works first appeared, and the supervision of which was his chief labour till his death in 1873.

His pastorate of St. John's took him down into the dens of the Cowgate, and stirred him up to do his utmost for the elevation of the degraded people who lived in them. Thus began his efforts for Ragged Schools. In the same line, he took up a work like that of Chalmers in the West Port, and was instrumental in rearing more than one church among the poor. It was in connection with such Evangelistic work that his sermons on "The City, its Sins and Sorrows," were first preached and published, and full details of the different departments of these enterprises will be found in the appendix to the early editions of these discourses. His energy as a philanthropist was equalled only by his earnestness in the pulpit.

As a preacher, he did not so much belong to any class as he constituted a whole class by himself. Since his appearance he has had many imitators, but when he rose to fame he was, in Great Britain at least, the only one of his kind. He was not an expository preacher, neither could he be called dogmatic or doctrinal. He did not deal very liberally either in what has been termed the hortatory method. But he was what Dr. McCosh has called him, " the pictorial preacher of his age."

In his earlier years he gave much attention to elocution. He believed that " the manner is to the matter as the powder is to the ball "; and he tells us that during his student life in Edinburgh "he attended elocution classes, winter after winter, walking across half the city and more, fair night and foul, and not getting back to his lodgings till about half-past ten. There he learned to find out and correct many acquired and more or less awkward defects in gesture—to be, in fact, natural; to acquire a command over his voice so as to suit its force and emphasis to the sense, and to modulate it so as to express the feelings, whether of surprise, or grief, or indignation, or pity." The wisdom of this course at that particular stage of his history was great. If he had deferred his lessons in elocution until after he had begun to preach he would have become stilted, self-conscious, and unnatural. But taking them just then, they passed into and became part of himself, so that he acted upon them unconsciously, and as it were automatically, and he thought no more about them when he was in the act of speaking than a practised writer does about spelling when he is in the heat of composition. If we wished to spoil a minister who is in actual work, we would send him to learn elocution; but if we wished to prepare a youth for doing effective work in the pulpit, we would take care that, while he is as yet, so to say, in the gristle, with his habits unset, he should be sent to a wise teacher to learn how to speak.

Dr. Guthrie's sermons were generally fully written out.* He set himself " to use the simplest and plainest terms, avoiding anything vulgar, but always, where possible, employing the Saxon tongue. He spared no pains, nor toil, nor time in making his descriptions graphic, his statements lucid, and his appeals pathetic." For years after his settlement in Edinburgh he spent three hours—those between six and nine in the morning—every day in ruminating on, digesting, and doing the utmost on his sermon. He wrote his discourse with his audience, in his imagination, before him. He even spoke aloud the words which he was inditing; thus, as it were, writing to his own dictation. After the sermon was finished he spent hours in correcting it, having left in later years for that purpose a blank page opposite every written one. His corrections consisted, as he has told us, in " cutting out dry bits, giving point to dull ones, making clear any obscurity, and narrative parts more graphic; throw-

---

* I have said generally, for I was informed recently by Dr. McCosh that he frequently, in the heat of utterance, put in passages which were not in the manuscript. But how he was able to resume his prepared discourse at the point at which he broke away to make such a digression is to me a mystery.

ing more pathos into appeals, and copying God in his works by adding the ornamental to the useful." The substance of the sermons, as we have said, was mainly pictorial. In his early preaching days at Arbirlot he had a young people's class, which assembled on the Sabbath evenings, and part of the exercise of the pupils was to give an account of the discourse which they had heard in the earlier part of the day. From the answers of the young people he discovered that they always remembered the illustrations best, and that determined him to give more attention to what he calls "the likes" in his discourses. It is noteworthy here that illustration was not originally his forte, but was acquired by steady, earnest, and persistent effort. Indeed, he went so far with it that at length the sermons came to be almost all illustration together.

And here is the place where the critic finds him most vulnerable. He overdid the pictorial. Very often the thing which he wanted to illustrate was forgotten in the wondrous beauty of his description of the illustration. In this respect there was a wide difference between him and his friend William Arnot,* greatly to the advantage of the latter.

---

* It is a mortification to me that I had to omit, owing to the time at my command for the delivery of these lectures,

Guthrie elaborated the illustration until it stood out a perfect word-painting before the eyes of the people ; Arnot flashed his simile for but a brief moment before the hearer, but the effect was to light up the whole subject, and that was all of which the audience was conscious. Neither of them was master of that use of the metaphor which was so characteristic of Bushnell, and which packs an illustration into a single word. That may sometimes be too condensed for effectiveness ; but Guthrie, on the other hand, was often too diffuse for the highest power. Besides, a sermon that is all illustration together cannot but be defective in instruction. In Guthrie's case it was fortunate that he had Dr. Hanna so long for a colleague, for that which was lacking in the one was plentifully supplied by the other, and the two were the " complements " of each other. Flowers are good, but we like a little fruit

---

any detailed reference to Mr. Arnot. He was a real genius. A rough diamond, but still a diamond. A clear head, a warm heart, an awkward yet strangely expressive manner, a fine fancy, strong common-sense, and pawkie humour were his outstanding peculiarities. He was the most Scotch of Scotchmen, but of him, too, it was true that he was best on the platform. The raciness and appropriateness of his anecdotes were equal to those of Guthrie. The one was all nature, the other's art had become natural.

as well; and though it be true, as Sir William Hamilton said, that Guthrie's illustrations had the force of logic which had only one step between the premise and the conclusion, yet a discourse that is all illustration will soon wither in the memory, and become as neglected as one of last week's bouquets.

In his delivery Dr. Guthrie preached *memoriter*. The "committing" of his discourses cost him little trouble. Even in his early days he wrote only one a week, and in some later years he was very far from accomplishing that; but his morning hours were abundantly sufficient to fix that in his mind, and "use so bred the habit in him" that latterly his memory retained his sermon almost without any effort of memorizing; so that when he was speaking he had nothing of the appearance of one who was remembering, but all the freedom, without any of the hesitancy or anxiety, of an extempore speaker. He was calm, self-possessed, deliberate, but rarely, if ever, impassioned. Intensely dramatic, he reproduced in action that which he was describing, often with such effect as to make the people forget that he was only describing. There is a passage in "The Gospel in Ezekiel" descriptive of the battle between David and Goliath, and

PULPITS OF DISSENTING CHURCHES. 265

one who heard it delivered told me that when the speaker launched the stone from the stripling's sling every one seated in the gallery opposite the pulpit dodged his head to elude the missile!

It was a remarkable audience that regularly worshipped in St. John's Free Church, Edinburgh, when Guthrie was in his power. There might have been seen, with his profuse whiskers, shaggy head, and plaided shoulders, Hugh Miller, the Cromarty stonemason, who became one of the foremost journalists and geologists of his day. Not far away was seated Dr. James Y. Simpson, the discoverer of chloroform, with his leonine face lighted up with interest as his eyes were fixed intently on the preacher. There too, sometimes, was the restless, erratic Blackie, Professor of Greek in the University, who came, as he said, to hear the most Homeric descriptions which this age has ever listened to. There, also, not seldom, right in front of the pulpit, was Lord Cockburn, the friend of Jeffrey and the favourite of all Scotland, whose delight it was to "have a greet wi' Guthrie." While he was able, too, the keen metaphysician, Sir William Hamilton, was occasionally seen within these homely walls; and week by week the passages were thronged with strangers from all quarters and from many lands, who timed their visits to the metropolis of Scotland so that they might be there on the Sabbath and " hear Guthrie."

What the results of such preaching were spiritually we are not able to say. We read little in the autobiography and memoir of conversions or growth in Christian character among the people that waited on his ministrations. This may, however, be largely owing to Scottish reticence on such subjects, and must not be taken as indicating that effects of that sort were few. But whatever else he secured, he gained and held the hearing of the people ; and if they were so ready to follow him—as we know they were—in his philanthropic schemes, we may well believe that many were led by him to choose " the good part that could not be taken from them."

But now our task is done, and I sum up my homiletic lessons for this whole review in two advices.

First, BE YOURSELVES. Pulpit efficiency is not a matter of method. There have been great preachers in all methods, with the paper and without it, extempore and memoriter, expository and topical. The efficiency is not in the method, but in the man.

As one has said, that which all great preachers have in common to make them great preachers "is, along with intellect, force of character, an energetic nature—will. A great preacher is not a mere artist, and not a feeble suppliant; he is a conquering soul, a monarch, a born ruler of mankind. He wills, and men bow."* Thus pulpit efficiency is only one of the forms of the efflorescence of character. Keep that in mind, and it will save you from the artificiality of imitation, while it will lead you to see that you will best cultivate homiletics through attention to character. Be yourselves, but make the best of yourselves, that you may be your highest selves.

And while you are thus careful to be yourselves DO NOT PREACH YOURSELVES. Preach Christ. Beware of hiding Him behind yourselves—rather hide yourselves behind Him; and while your audience hear the voice, let them "see no man but Jesus only." Do not make the sermon an end—use it only as a means; and let your end be, not the gathering of a multitude, nor the making of a name for yourselves, but the saving

---

* "Lectures on the History of Preaching," p. 119. John A. Broadus, D.D.

of them that hear you, and then you will not lack success.

It has been a joy to me to come once more thus closely into fellowship with you and your teachers, but the most joyful thing of all is that now my work is done. Nay, that is not the most joyful thing, after all; for it will be the highest of all joy to me to know that I have done anything, however small, to quicken your enthusiasm for that noble work to which you have given yourselves, or that I have laid up in you some memories which you can recall when haply he who has addressed you has passed within the veil to the companionship of those of whom he has been honoured to speak in the midst of you.

INDEX.

ALEXANDER, Rev. W. L., D.D., LL.D., quoted from or referred to, 24, 28, 245; biography of Dr. Wardlaw by, characterized, 245; characteristics of, as a preacher, 246-250
Anderson, Rev. William, LL.D., 23; as a preacher, 239-241
Anne, Queen, patronage enactment under, 15
Anti-burghers, the, 20
Anti-papal period of Scottish Church History, 7
Anti-patronage period of Scottish Church History, 8-15
Anti-prelatic period of Scottish Church History, 9-15
Arnot, Rev. William, 262

BAPTIST churches in Scotland, 28
Baxter, Richard, on Rutherfurd's Letters, 81
Bayne, Dr. Peter, quoted from, 181
Binning, Hugh, referred to, 120
Blackie, Professor, 266
Blaikie, Rev. Dr. W. G., quoted, 116, 117
Blair, Dr. Hugh, 17, 144-150
Blair, Rev. Robert, 85
Boston, Rev. Thomas, 150-154
Boston, Rev. Thomas, jun., 21
Breda, declaration of Charles the Second at, 109
Brown, Rev. John, of Haddington, 228
Brown, Rev. John, Whitburn, 227

Brown, Rev. John, D.D., 23 ; remarks of, on Leighton, 124 ;
on Maclaurin, 158; characteristics of, as a preacher, 229

Brown, John, M.D., description of Chalmers by, 215-219;
referred to, 228, 229

Buchanan, Rev. Dr. Robert, 18

Burghers, the, 20

Burnet, Bishop, quoted from, 109, 120

Burns, Robert, 5, 6, 13, 97

CAIRD, Rev. Principal, 60

Cairns, Rev. Principal, 60

Cameron, Richard, 13, 61, 130; sermon by, 131

Cameronians, the, 18, 221

Campbell, Sir Hugh, quoted, 93

Candlish, Rev. Dr. R. S., 18, 255-257

Cargil, Donald, 13

Carlyle, Rev. Dr. Alexander, 18, 150

Carlyle, Thomas, 32, 201, 211

Caution, Scottish, 5

Cecil, Richard, on Rutherfurd's Letters, 81

Chalmers, Rev. Dr. Thomas, 17, 60, 184-219; astronomical discourses of, 198; influence of, as a theological professor, 215;
work of, in the West Port, 207 ; characteristics of, 211-219

Characteristics of the Scottish People, 2-7

Charles the First, 9, 11, 72, 106

Charles the Second, 12, 73, 106, 110

Clarendon, Lord, on Alexander Henderson, 76

Cockburn, Lord, 49, 265

Coleridge on Leighton's Calvinism, 116

Congregationalism, Scottish, origin of, 28

Conventicles, open-air, description of, 128

Covenant, the National, 11, 76

Covenant, the Solemn League and, 11, 105, 106

Cromwell, Oliver, 11, 12, 73, 83

INDEX.

Cunningham, Rev. Dr. John, referred to, 69
Curriculum of Scottish students for the ministry, 31

DICK, Rev. John, D.D., 23, 225
Dickson, Rev. David, 85, 87-94; scholarship and education of, 102
Disruption of Scottish Church, 17
Dourness, Scottish, 4

EADIE, Rev. John, D.D., LL.D., quoted from, 81, 158; characteristics of, 232-235
Education of early Scottish ministers, 102
Edwards, Jonathan, Scottish correspondence of, 160, 163; influence of, on Chalmers, 186
Erskine, Rev. Ebenezer, 19, 23, 154-157
Erskine, Rev. Dr. John, 18, 162; description of, by Sir Walter Scott, 163
Erskine, Rev. Ralph, 23, 154-157, 167
Evangelical Union, the, 29
Evangelicals, the, some characteristics of, 165; lessons from, 169, 170

FAIRFOWL, Archbishop, 106, 107
Ferguson, Alexander, Lieutenant-Colonel, quoted, 113
Finlayson, James, D.D., quoted, 145
Fleming's "Fulfilling of the Scriptures," quoted from, 91, 98
Foster, John, referred to, 167
Free Church of Scotland, the, 17
Fuller, Andrew, on Chalmers, 214

GEDDES, Jenny, 9, 10, 72
Gillespie, George, 11
Gillespie, Thomas, 21

Glasgow Act, the, 106
Grahame's, James, "The Sabbath," quoted from, 137
Grosart, Rev. Dr. A. B., quoted, 82, 86
Guthrie, Rev. Dr. Thomas, 18, 255, 257-266

HADOW, Principal, 152
Haldane, James A., 25, 27
Haldane, Robert, 25, 27
Hall, Robert, criticism of, on Chalmers, 213
Hamilton, Bishop, 106
Hamilton, Patrick, 7
Hamilton, Sir William, 264, 265
Hampden, John, 10
Hanna, Rev. Dr. William, Life of Chalmers by, quoted from, 192-195, 200, 202, 209; colleague of Guthrie, 263
Henderson, Rev. Alexander, 11, 63, 70-78; sermons of, 73; prayers of, 73
Hetherington's "History of the Church of Scotland," quoted from, 92, 98
Homiletic lessons, 266, 267
Hoppin, Rev. Professor, 197
Hume, David, 26, 150, 181

INDEPENDENCE a characteristic of Scotchmen, 2
Innes, Mr. Taylor, quoted, 83
Intensity a characteristic of Scotchmen, 3
Irving, Rev. Edward, 201, 203

JAMES THE SIXTH, 9, 65, 106
Jeffrey, Lord, 49, 212

KEBLE, John, quoted, 149
Ker, Rev. John, D.D., 23
Kilmany, Chalmers's address on leaving, 192-197
"Kilmarnock, History of," by A. McKay, referred to, 127

King, Rev. David, LL.D., characteristics of, as a preacher, 235-237

Knox, John, 71, 37-62; influence of, on Scottish pulpit, 57-62; characteristics of, as a preacher, 44-57; description of, by James Melville, 52; Witherspoon a descendant of, 161

LAUD, Archbishop, 9, 11

Lawson, Rev. Dr. George, 23, 228

Leighton, Archbishop, 13, 63, 105, 112-138

Literary services of the Moderates to Scotland, 181

Livingstone, Rev. John, 94-99; learning of, 95

Lockhart's, J. G., "Peter's Letters to his Kinsfolk," quoted from or referred to, 97, 172

MCCOSH, Dr. James, quoted from or referred to, 15, 16, 156, 261

McCrie, Rev. Dr. Thomas (the elder), quoted from or referred to, 53, 65, 67, 153, 173; characteristics of, as a preacher, 225-227

McCrie, Rev. Dr. Thomas (the younger), quoted from or referred to, 69, 71, 85, 86

Maclaurin, John, 18, 157-161

Macleod, Dr. Norman, characteristics of, as a preacher, 250-255

"Marrow of Modern Divinity, The," 152

Mason, Rev. John, 162

Melville, Andrew, 9, 63-70, 102

Melville, James, description of John Knox by, 52; description of Glasgow University by, 64

Merchant, an English, description of Blair, Rutherfurd, and Dickson by, 85

Middleton, Earl of, 107

Miller, Hugh, quoted from or referred to, 163, 165, 225, 226, 265

Milton, John, quoted from or referred to, 83, 112
Missions, debate on, in 1796, 165
Moderates, the, 24, 36, 139-165; literary eminence of, 181
Moncreiff, Lord, 171
Moncreiff, Sir Henry, 17, 162
Morison, Rev. Dr. James, 29, 235
Morton, Regent, 61, 67

NATIONAL Covenant, the, 11; signing of, 72

"OLD MORTALITY," ministerial characters in, 126, 127
Outed ministers, the, 108

PATON, Captain John, 126
Patronage law enacted, 17; abolished, 18
Peden, Alexander, quoted from, 133
Peter's "Letters to his Kinsfolk," by J. G. Lockhart, quoted from or referred to, 97, 172
Poetic sense in Scotchmen, 4
Protesters and Resolutioners, 101
Psalms, Scottish metrical version of the, 129
Pulpit and national character, connection between, 1

RAINY, Rev. Robert, D.D., quoted from, 142
Ramsay, Dean, 5
Reformed Presbyterian Church, 221
Relief Church, 21; characteristics of its preachers, 237-241
Renwick, James, 13
Resolutioners and Protesters, 101
Restoration of the Stuarts, 12
Reticence of the Scotch on religious subjects, 6
Revolution settlement of Scottish Church, 13-17
Robertson, Dr. James, Errol, 32
Robertson, Rev. Principal, 17, 163, 181

INDEX.

Rough, John, 40
Russell, Rev. David, 241
Rutherfurd, Samuel, 11, 60, 63, 79-87; letters of, 81; works of, 81; anecdote of Usher and, 100, 101

SCOTT, Sir Walter, quoted from, 163; referred to, 126
Scottish characteristics, 1-6
Scottish Ecclesiastical History, summary of, 7-33
Secession, first, from the Scottish Church, 19; second, 21; third, 21
Shairp, Principal, 97
Sharpe, Archbishop, 106
Shotts, Kirk of, sermon by Livingstone at the, 96-99
Simpson, Patrick, quoted, 85
Simpson, Robert, D.D., 110, 130
Simpson, Sir James Y., 265
Smith, Rev. Walter C., D.D., quoted, 120
Society-men, the, 18; union of, with Free Church, 19, 222
Solemn League and Covenant, 11, 105, 106
Stanley, Dean, 69, 100, 139, 142
"Stewarton Sickness, The," 91
Stuarts, character of the, 109
Symington, William, D.D., 222

TERROT, Bishop, anecdote of, 20
Thomson, Dr. Andrew, 18, 166; characteristics of, 170-180; great speech of, on immediate emancipation, 177; connection of, with Chalmers, 189
"Tulchan" bishops, 8, 9

UNITED Presbyterian Church, 22; curriculum of study in, 31; Declaratory Statement of, as to subscription to Standards, 34
United Secession Church, 21
Usher, Archbishop, anecdote of, and Rutherfurd, 82, 100

WALKER, Rev. James, D.D., quoted from or referred to, 80, 93, 96
Walker, Rev. N. L., quoted, 12, 205
Wardlaw, Rev. Ralph, D.D., 28; description of Chalmers by, 198, 199; characteristics of, as a preacher, 242-246
Watson, Jean L., quoted from, 173, 174, 176
Welsh, John, 9
Westminster Assembly of Divines, 11, 72, 80
Wilks, Matthew, 25
Wishart, George, 7, 38
Witherspoon, John, D.D., 16, 161

THE END.

Other Solid Ground Classic Reprints

The following titles are available on preaching and pastoral ministry:

Homiletics & Pastoral Theology by William G.T. Shedd

W.G.T.Shedd expounds almost every aspect of preaching, analyzing its nature, outlining the main features which should characterize powerful preaching and describing the approach, plan, actual construction and refinements of a sermon. This volume was used for many years as a standard textbook in several theological seminaries throughout the U.S.

A History of Preaching by Edwin Charles Dargan

This two volume hardcover set, first published in 1905, was written as a tribute to Dargan's homiletics professor at Southern Baptist Theological Seminary, John A. Broadus. Dargan later became a colleague and then the successor to Broadus in the chair of Homiletics at SBTS in Louisville, KY. The inspiration for these volumes came from the yearly "delightful lectures on the History of Preaching" from Broadus. "Under his inspiring teaching my interest as a student was awakened in the subject, and when years afterward it fell to me first to share his labors of instruction and then to succeed them, I became more and more deeply interested in the historical part of the course in homiletics."

The Preacher and His Models by James Stalker

This volume consists of the 9 lectures delivered in 1891 at The Yale Lectures on Preaching. Appended to the volume is a sermon Stalker preached at an Ordination Service in 1879. It was Alexander Whyte who encouraged the publication of that sermon when it was first delivered. After an Introductory Lecture, Stalker then divides his subject into four lectures using the Old Testament Prophets as examples, and then four lectures on the New Testament Apostles. As with all of Stalker's works there is both light and heat upon every page.

Lectures on the History of Preaching by John A. Broadus

John A. Broadus (1827-1895) delivered these five lectures in May of 1876 at Newton Theological Institute near Boston, and they immediately caused a stir of interest for their publication. It was lectures like these which later moved his student E.C. Dargan to desire to spend his life studying the history of preaching. This eventually led Dargan to write his two volume massive work on "A History of Preaching" listed above.

Call us toll free at **1-877-666-9469**
E-mail us at **sgcb@charter.net**
Visit our web site at **solid-ground-books.com**

www.ingramcontent.com/pod-product-compliance
Lightning Source LLC
Chambersburg PA
CBHW031620160426
43196CB00006B/208